BUSINESS GROWTH
DAY BY DAY

38 Lessons Every Entrepreneur Must Learn to Get More Done and Make More Money

MATTHEW PAULSON

Published by American Consumer News, LLC.

First edition: August 2016

ISBN-10:0-9905300-3-5
ISBN-13:978-0-9905300-3-9

Editing and Cover Design: Rebecca McKeever
Book Design: James Woosley (FreeAgentPress.com)

AUDIO BONUS:

By purchasing this book, you will receive a collection of five bonus audio interviews that I have participated in that relate to growing and scaling businesses.

In order to get access to these audio interviews, visit:

mattpaulson.com/bgbonus

If you have any trouble accessing your book bonuses, feel free to reach out to me at:

mattpaulson.com/contact

TABLE OF CONTENTS

INTRODUCTION

First-time entrepreneurs make a lot of mistakes. They spend too much time on their product and not enough time on marketing. They waste energy on things like business cards and logos that don't contribute to the growth of their business. They fail to organize their finances in any meaningful way. They don't put in enough hours to actually get their business off the ground. Almost every entrepreneur makes these kind of mistakes when they are first getting started, and I was no exception.

My company, MarketBeat.com, now generates millions of dollars in revenue each year and reaches hundreds of thousands of readers on a daily basis, but it wasn't always that way. When I began my business in 2006, I had no formal business education, no actual business experience and only a vague idea of how to get my business off the ground. The original business model of MarketBeat.com was to operate a network of personal finance blogs. I probably spent a month picking out the name "Getting Green" as the name of my blog, only to change the name to American Consumer News several months later. I didn't bother incorporating the business or setting up any kind of accounting system at all. I spent far too much time working in my business as an employee and not nearly enough time working on my business as the owner.

The biggest mistake I made was incorporating as an S-Corp without realizing what tax and payroll implications came along with that. When your business operates as an S-Corp, you are supposed to hire yourself as an employee and run payroll. The lawyer that set up my S-Corp neglected to tell me that and I neglected to run payroll for the first two years of my business. Eventually, I figured out the mistake I had made and had to go back and refile the last three years of my corporate and personal tax returns. I ended up paying about $4,000 in back taxes and fees to the accountant that had to rerun all of my returns.

Given the number of early mistakes I made in my business, I questioned whether or not I was cut out to be an entrepreneur. It wasn't until I began really getting involved in my local business community in 2013 that I realized that just about everyone makes the same mistakes when they are first starting their businesses. I got so fired up by some of the mistakes that first-time entrepreneurs make and the misconceptions that they have that I started writing about them on my blog at mattpaulson.com.

It didn't take long for me to realize that I really enjoyed writing about entrepreneurship. Over the past four years, I've written 3 books and more than 100 articles on entrepreneurship and personal finance. My first book, *40 Rules for Internet Business Success* (40rulesbook.com), teaches the principles and strategies that I've used to grow my businesses. My second book, *Email Marketing Demystified* (myemailmarketingbook.com), provides a comprehensive guide for any entrepreneur to integrate email marketing into their business. My third book, *The Ten-Year Turnaround*, teaches readers how they can grow their income and achieve financial freedom in ten years or less.

What to Expect from *Business Growth Day by Day*

This book is a compilation of some of the short-form articles I've published on my blog in the last several years. My assistant Rebecca McKeever and I went through all of the articles that I've written about entrepreneurship during the last five years and have selected 38 articles that offer helpful lessons of entrepreneurship and share my unique perspective on how to run a business. We have gone through and cleaned up each article and organized them chronologically.

There are chapters about a wide variety of business topics, including marketing, personal finance, personal networking, sales, online business, productivity and business failure. While this book broaches a number of different subjects, my hope is that you will take something away from each chapter and become a better entrepreneur as a result.

Who Should Read *Business Growth Day by Day*

This book is primarily written for entrepreneurs and business people with an entrepreneurial mindset that want to get better at what they do. If you desire personal growth and want to grow your business, many of the chapters in this book will be beneficial to you. *Business Growth Day by Day* is written very much in the same vein as my first book, *40 Rules for Internet Business Success*. If you enjoyed the entrepreneurial perspective and the bite-sized chapters in that book, you will also enjoy *Business Growth Day by Day*.

How to Read *Business Growth Day by Day*

This book is intended to be read over the course of 38 days. Since this book discusses a wide variety of topics, I suggest that you read one chapter every morning until you have completed the book.

After you read a chapter, spend some time during the day thinking about the content in that chapter.

- Do you agree with my viewpoint on that particular topic?
- Can you implement any of the advice in the chapter in your business?
- Is there anyone that you know that can benefit from the advice in the chapter?

While it would be easy for many readers to knock out this book in a couple of hours, I strongly encourage you to read this book like a daily devotional in order to get the maximum value out of it.

To Your Future Success

Whether you're a seasoned entrepreneur or are just getting started and are still making a lot of mistakes, my hope is that the concepts and strategies outlined in the chapters of *Business*

Growth Day by Day will help you become a better entrepreneur and run a more successful business. I can't promise that you'll be successful, but by the end of this book, you'll have a clear understanding of how I think about business and the strategies and tactics that I've used to build multiple six-figure and seven-figure businesses.

1

Five Common Website Mistakes Made by Small Businesses

If you're a small business owner, you know that your company probably needs a website. So, you ask around to know if anyone knows a good website developer. You find a consultant or an agency, write them a check and have them build you a website that makes use of the latest software and design trends. You've got a fancy new website, with all of your company's information listed. Mission accomplished, right?

Not so fast. Like all components of a business, your website must be maintained over time and optimized to get the best marketing results. There are several major mistakes that small business owners tend to make with their websites.

Don't repeat these frequently-made mistakes made by small business owners:

1. **Not Having a Consistent Strategy**

   Your website should not be a general electronic brochure about your company. Your website should have a single major purpose, such as attracting new customers. All of your website's content and design elements should revolve around the strategy and purpose of your website. If your website's goal is to attract new customers, it should have up-to-date, quality information about your company's products or services and contain a clear call-to-action to get potential customers to call you or fill out an opt-in form on your website.

2. **Not Updating Your Website**

   Websites are not fine wines. They do not get better with age. Information becomes stale. Technologies become out of date. Design trends change. You should review your website on a quarterly basis to make sure the information about your company is still up-to-date. You should expect to revamp your website every four to five years. If you haven't created a new version of your website since 2007, it might be time to bring on a web developer to do a refresh.

3. **Ignoring Software Updates and Backups**

   If your website was built in the last few years, it's probably powered by a content management system, such as WordPress, Drupal or Joomla. This software needs to be updated on a regular basis using the built-in update tool that comes with your content management system or through the assistance of your web developer. Failing to keep your content management system up-to-date will leave your website vulnerable to being hacked.

The other major technical component you need to make sure is being taken care of is backups. Don't automatically assume that your web developer is backing up your website or that your hosting provider is backing up your website either. If possible, use an automatic script to perform weekly backups of your website and its associated database. Your web developer should be able to set this up for you.

4. Failing to Use Email Marketing

If someone ends up on your website, there's a strong possibility that they're a potential customer. If you're not trying to collect the email addresses of people that visit your website, you're throwing money out the window. One of the best ways to keep your business fresh in someone's mind is to email them several times over the course of a few weeks. Consider adding an opt-in box to your website that allows someone to sign up for a free email newsletter or email course that's sent out over a period of a few weeks. This may sound like a burdensome task, but it can all be set up automatically using email collection and autoresponder software, such as MailChimp or Drip.

5. Forgetting to Market Your Website

If you build it, there's no guarantee that anyone will come. If you do nothing, your website might eventually get indexed by search engines and you'll get a trickle of traffic from people searching for your business specifically, but that's about it. To get the best return on your website, you need to develop a comprehensive marketing strategy for your website that includes search engine optimization (building links to your website and optimizing your website for the right keywords), social media, email marketing and some form of advertising (depending on your industry).

Have you made any of these mistakes with your website? If so, what action steps are you going to take to resolve the issue?

2

A Sure-Fire Way to Limit Your Business's Upside Potential

What's the difference between a food-service employee and a high-price attorney? When it comes to their compensation structure, not all that much. Both offer to perform specific tasks for an hourly rate. Granted, an attorney can charge a much higher hourly rate for their services than a fast food employee can, but both the attorney and the fast food employee severely limit their income potential because they can only work so many hours in a week.

Move Away from Hourly Billing

If you're in business and are providing your services at an hourly rate, you need to stop. Even if you could bill out your entire week for fifty weeks a year and could command an hourly rate of $100 an hour, the most you would ever possibly make is $200,000 per year. That might seem like a lot of money to some, but the second you stop working, you stop making money. The freedom to spend more time with your family that you were hoping for becomes much less possible because you've become a slave to the billable hour. Your business is not sellable because it's entirely dependent upon you doing the work and, let's be honest, $200,000 per year is not all that great of an upside potential for a person that takes on the risk of becoming a business owner. Ideally, you'd make quite a bit more than that after several years of hard work.

Per-Project Billing

Instead of trading your time for money (billing hourly), trade a specific set of results for a pre-agreed upon amount of money. By billing on a per-project basis, your client knows exactly what they're going to be paying for your service and you have the flexibility to deliver the result using the most efficient means possible. Your incentive is no longer to use the most billable hours you can without getting in trouble with your client. Rather, your incentive becomes to complete your client's project in the most efficient, leveraged manner.

By moving to a payment-per-specific-result model, you also have the ability to build a system of people, business processes and technology that deliver the end result the customer desires. If you build a solid enough system, you can work yourself out of a job or at least have the ability to take as much time off as you'd like. By having a delivery system in place that does not rely on you, your business becomes increasingly scalable to larger volumes and becomes much more sellable to a potential buyer.

Here's an example from my website development consulting business:

If someone is paying me to build them a website, I could spend a bunch of time doing the design work, the HTML/CSS/JavaScript work, content management system setup and content migration. I might work 50 hours on a project and make $5,000 for my time at $100 an hour. Alternatively, I can charge the client $5,000 for the project, farm out the design work to a freelancer for about $1,000 and have my assistant do the content migration from the client's current website (say, 5-10 hours at ~$20 or so an hour). I might put 10 hours into the same project and have $1,200 in expenses. I might not have made as much on the project as if I did all of the work myself ($5,000 vs. $3,800), but my hourly rate on the project jumped from $100 per hour to $380 per hour. I've also freed up a bunch of time in the process. By working on a per-project basis and leveraging the talents and abilities of others, I have the ability to take on more projects or work much less.

I'm Sold. Now What?

There are really only two action steps to take once you've decided to give up on the hourly grind of a consulting business. The first is obvious, quit billing hourly and start billing customers based on a pre-agreed upon price for a specific set of results. If they end up about what they would have been paying otherwise, it will be a wash and no one will likely complain about it.

The second step is to start finding people, processes and technology that can you can leverage to start building a system to deliver your products or services. What aspects of your service do you hate doing, aren't any good at, or otherwise don't want to do? Start with those and find other ways to get that work done. This might mean hiring a freelancer or virtual assistant to help you with some aspects of projects. It might mean farming it out to another company or leveraging software or other equipment in a new way. Your long term goal should be to have a product delivery system that does not rely on you personally. If you build your system well, you'll end up with more time, freedom, and (hopefully) a much better bottom line.

3

There's Only One Problem with Passive Income Businesses

If you've spent more than a minute hanging out on internet marketing forums or paying attention to gurus, you've been pitched on the idea of generating a passive income stream. In order to get you to sign up for a service or buy some sort of product, some marketer will sell you on the dream that you can build an easy-to-set-up business that will generate income for you while you're doing just about everything but working. And of course, they'll teach you how to set up these passive, income-generating businesses for just $39.97 (of course, if you really want to learn their secret, you'll also have to join their private mastermind group for $99.00 per month).

The dream is that you have some sort of business that runs around the clock without your intervention. Hanging out on the beach? You're making money. Taking a nap? You're making money. Having dinner? You're making money. In the shower? You're making money. Your passive income business may be a website that generates ad revenue from Google AdSense. It might be an e-commerce store with outsourced fulfillment. It could be a collection of ebooks that you sell through your website. Anything that doesn't require you to be at your computer while you're making money could be considered a passive income business.

There's only one problem with passive income businesses. They don't actually exist.

There are many entrepreneurs that have businesses that generate income while they sleep, but there's nothing passive about them. **The idea that you can create a business that you only work on a few hours per week that generates significant amounts of income for you is a fairy tale. The mythical 4-*Hour Workweek* does not exist.** There's nothing passive about building businesses that generate passive income streams. The reality is that successful business owners with "passive income" businesses work really, really hard on their business to generate income when they're not working. They are compulsive about finding ways to improve and grow their business. Chances are, they are working harder than you do. How do you think they got where they are? Do you think Pat Flynn built a business that generates $50,000 per month in affiliate commissions by working four hours per week? Do you think that Tim Ferris built the "four-hour" brand by working four hours per week? Not a chance.

Yes, you can build your business in such a way that you get paid when you're not working. I'm living proof. Seven years into building my online business, I can take a day off just about whenever I want and not skip a beat. The problem is that it will never happen if you start off only working a handful of hours per week. You'll never get anywhere because you didn't do any work up front. The occasional four-hour workweek is a luxury for people that have already put thousands of hours of work into building their businesses. If you're just starting your business, you need to put as much ambition and effort into building and growing your business as possible. If you truly want to have a business that generates passive income, be prepared to put in thousands of hours of work to make that happen.

4

Don't Build an Ecosystem-Based Business

In the last five years, there has been a major trend to build businesses on top of the platforms offered by major web companies, such as eBay, Facebook, Twitter, Apple (iTunes) and Google (YouTube, Search). Eight years ago, the big thing was to build an eBay business. Four years ago, the big thing to do was build a Twitter client or a Facebook application. More recently, the big thing to do has been to build apps and get distribution from Apple's AppStore and the Google Play Store.

Working inside of an established ecosystem, such as iTunes, YouTube or Facebook allows you to tap into an established user base, but doing so places your business at significant risk. **When you piggyback off the platform of a major company, your business only continues to exist as long as it suits the company whose platform you're building off of.** When the platform you're working on decides they don't need you anymore, you're toast.

When Twitter decided that it only wanted users to use its official software clients, it made changes to its API that made it more difficult for third party Twitter clients to operate. It stopped promoting them in its feed and has publicly warned developers not to build new Twitter clients. When Facebook revamped the functionality of Facebook Pages to make use of the Timeline, third party developers that relied on the ability to put custom content on the homepage of a Facebook Page were pushed out of Facebook's ecosystem. There are dozens of stories of developers getting removed from Apple's AppStore for running afoul of arbitrary rules, such as AppGratis.

There's a common saying in online business, and that's "the money's in the customer list." In other words, **your future ability to generate income is based on the relationship you have with your customers and your ability to contact them.** If you're working inside of an ecosystem, your list only exists as long as that ecosystem exists and as long as you stay in the good graces of that ecosystem. If your account gets shut-down or a social network suddenly changes the game, you lose your ability to talk to your customers.

A while back, Facebook decided that it would charge commercial operators of Facebook Pages to communicate with their customers, and Mark Cuban famously abandoned Facebook as a marketing tool. If you have a major following on Facebook, but suddenly have to pay a significant sum of money to post a message to them where they'll actually see it, your company's future ability to generate income is constrained significantly.

The moral of the story is that **you need to own your customer list.** You shouldn't rely on having a big following on social media, a bunch of subscribers in YouTube or a large base of installs of your app. You need to have the email address of each of your customers (or mailing address and phone number) so that you can contact them in the future regardless of the status of any social network or other ecosystem. Social networks come and go, but email addresses and physical addresses rarely change.

If you own your customer list and have the email addresses of your customer base, you will always be able to generate more income in the future, even if Google, Apple, Facebook or Twitter decide they don't need you anymore. You can always let your customer list know about the next project you're working on or find some related product or service to market to them. **The ongoing business relationship should be between you and your customers.** Don't let Facebook, Twitter, Google or Apple get in your way.

5

Eight Strategies for Email Marketing Success

My company, American Consumer News, LLC, sends out about two million emails per month (as of Fall 2013). The vast majority of these are the daily edition of our investment newsletter, ARN Daily. We do send out our fair share of marketing messages too, so I've had a lot of opportunities to try things out to see what generally works and what doesn't.

Here are eight email marketing strategies I've had success with:

1. Be Personal

Avoid using your company name as the "from name" in your emails. Use your name, or the name of the person that will be responding to the emails. I also suggest starting your emails off using "Hi [name] –", or just "Hi –", and using a conversational tone throughout the letter. Use "you" and "your" language where possible. Making your marketing messages more personal will decrease the likelihood your users dismiss your message as an advertisement they're not interested in and will increase the likelihood that they actually read your email.

2. Have a Clear Call to Action

At the bottom of your email, you should have a single, clear call to action, such as "Click Here to Download Your Copy of [X]". I generally recommend letting this call to action be on a line of its own below the last sentence of your message and above your signature line. I also recommend having a secondary call to action below your email signature and adding another link to your landing page somewhere in the body of the message.

3. Be Repetitive

Just because you think about your company's products and services on a daily basis doesn't mean your customers do. When you send out an important email marketing message, consider sending it again a week later to the list of people that didn't open the initial message. Alternatively, use a series of emails that all drive home the same message or call to action. I'll frequently do three or four emails over the course of two weeks if I really want to make sure my readers get the message.

4. **Use Single Purpose Messages**
   If you want your audience to do something (i.e. download your report, sign-up for a free trial, or anything like that), that should be the only thing in your email. The only two choices your users should have is to (A) delete your email or (B) move forward with your single call to action.

5. **Avoid Image Heavy Templates**
   Most email clients will disable images by default and require the user to click a button to enable images for your emails. I find it's best to use a simple template, or no template at all in your emails. Email is a text-based medium, so do your selling with your copy. Don't rely on an image heavy template to do your sales that many of your users won't ever see.

6. **Be Creative**
   Make use of creative subject lines and openers in your email messages. Use short subject lines that engage the reader like "Strange Question?", "Important (please read)" or "Bad News." Leaving the reader with some level of intrigue in the subject line will make them more likely to open the message than if the subject line gives away the entirety of the message. Of course, you won't be able to get away with using subject lines like "Bad news…" every time, but every now and then, they can be a big winner. Furthermore, try to make your messages as fun and interesting to read as possible. Your readers already get enough boring marketing email.

7. **Manage Your IP and Domain Reputation**

Your domain name and the IP address you send email from has a reputation on the internet whether you know it or not. The reputation of your mail server and your domain name will determine whether or not your messages end up in someone's spam folder. Use blacklist checkers like MxToolbox, DNSBL and SenderScore to check the reputation of your domain name and IP address. If you find yourself on a blacklist, typically the list manager will have a form you'll need to fill out to remove yourself from the list. I recommend checking your domain and IP address's reputation at least monthly.

8. **Track Your Results**

For every marketing email you send out, you need to be able to track the results that came from that specific email. You should know how many people opened it, how many people clicked through to your landing page and how many people completed the action on your landing page you wanted them to take. Ideally, you'll know what the total value of revenue came from each email sent. If you can clearly connect revenue with the marketing emails you send out, you'll be able to identify a pattern over time of the types of emails that work best for your reader base.

Of course, the strategies that will do well for you will vary some based on your audience. What works well for my audience may not work well for yours. You'll want to test my recommendations against what you're doing now by running split-tests or otherwise segmenting your audience.

6

How to Level Up in Online Business

If you were to do a search for the keyword "make money online", you would get back thousands of websites that would teach you to build start-from-nothing businesses, such as long-tail AdSense websites, strategies to generate revenue with affiliate marketing and blueprints to make money with Facebook or Twitter. Many people in online business get started doing these types of things, but they rarely ever generate significant amounts of wealth.

Level-One Businesses

I call these level-one business models. They don't take much to get started because you're making use of other company's resources and platforms. There are a lot of people using these business models, some successfully and some not and you generally don't have a community or subscriber base built around your business. You might make some amount of money with these types of business models, but they very rarely scale up to four or five figures in monthly revenue. Some notable examples of successful level-one businesses include Pat Flynn's Security Guard Training website and Spencer Haws' Best Survival Knife Guide website.

Why Not to Build a Level-One Business

There are three major issues with level-one business models. First, there are no barriers to entry. It costs almost nothing to build a website that you hope will get search traffic from Google that will turn into ad dollars. Anyone that can read a few guides online, put some time in and do very basic website development work can build a network of niche AdSense websites. Because there are no barriers to entry, there's a ton of competition. Not only are you competing with other would-be entrepreneurs, you're also competing with major, established brands for search traffic. You're just one more website in Google's massive search index and aren't likely to generate a significant income without a substantial amount of content development and marketing work.

Second, you're wholly dependent upon someone else's ecosystem when you're building a level-one business. When Facebook decided it was going to charge publishers to reach the audience of their Facebook fan pages, many entrepreneurs' business models stopped working overnight. When Google added the Panda and Penguin algorithms to their ranking system, many people stopped receiving any meaningful amount of search traffic overnight. There are thousands of occurrences where an affiliate program changed their rules or payout structure and people that were making large amounts of money lost their income stream overnight. When your business is totally reliant on another company whose interests aren't necessarily aligned with yours, you're asking for trouble.

Finally, you generally don't have a customer list or a user community with level-one businesses. People will come to your website from Google, read your article and hopefully click through to a contextual ad-banner or an affiliate link to Amazon. You never collect the ability to contact them again in the future by way of email or have an active community surrounding your business. Because you can't independently contact your audience outside of whatever traffic method you've latched onto, you're even more dependent upon Facebook, Twitter, Pinterest or Google to keep your business going. Companies that have customer lists and user communities are far more sustainable than those that don't, because they can always rely on their existing customer list for revenue, even if search engines and social media sites stop sending them web traffic.

The Anatomy of a Level-Two Business

If the gold miners of the 19th century were entrepreneurs with level-one business models, the people that sold canvas tents, blue jeans, shovels and mining picks to miners had level-two business models. Equipment suppliers had a steady customer base of miners and made use of skills to do things that only a handful of people could do. Anyone could become a gold miner, but selling mining and camping equipment required manufacturing, importation, marketing and sales skills. These people generally did far better than the boom-or-bust gold miners of the 19th century. Their businesses were more stable, relatively predictable and had real barriers to entry.

Level-two businesses make use of personal skills and abilities, have some form of barrier to entry, don't rely on a single platform for traffic and revenue and result in the building of a community or customer list. Examples of level-two businesses include e-commerce stores, membership websites and software-as-a-service (SaaS) businesses.

How to Build a Level-Two Business

If you want to graduate beyond a level-one business, you need to start looking at more complex business models that not everyone can do. Take inventory of your unique skills and abilities and try to identify businesses that would make use of your personal strengths. If you have audio or video production skills, you might offer a service that does Podcast or video production. If you have significant knowledge about a certain trade, skill or hobby, you might offer consulting services, a paid email newsletter or a membership website. If you can write software and have a good mind for business processes, you might build a SaaS business. You don't necessarily have to be passionate about the level-two business you're building, but you should have some skills that will contribute to the growth of your business. The key is to find a business model that you can do that has meaningful barriers to entry in the form of required skills or resources.

Your level-two business should have a steady and reliable means of contacting prospective customers independent of Apple, Amazon, Facebook, Google, Microsoft, Pinterest or Twitter. This might mean you're cold calling other small businesses, using direct mail, doing guest blogging, engaging in email marketing or offering to be a guest on other people's podcasts. Alternatively, you can make use of the big-traffic sending platforms if you have multiple traffic sources. If you're getting customers from Bing, Google, your iPhone/iPad app, Facebook, Twitter and Amazon, you're a lot more diversified than if you're just getting sales through Amazon or traffic through Google. You should have your marketing strategy figured out before you start building your product or service, because the best product or service in the world won't do anyone any good if they don't know about it.

Finally, your level-two business should result in you building a database of subscribers/customers (preferably in the form of email addresses) that you can contact in the future. Ideally, there will be some sort of community that exists surrounding your business as well. If you have a list of subscribers or customers, you have the ability to maintain a relationship with them and sell to them again in the future, regardless of your standing with search engines and social media platforms.

My Transition from a Level-One Business to Multiple Level-Two Businesses

When I started in online business in 2007, I created a few personal finance websites. They made about five thousand dollars per month at their peak in ad-revenue. They did okay. Unfortunately, there were hundreds of other personal finance bloggers doing the same thing. I probably wasn't going to be the guy that stood above the rest of the crowd and to be honest, they weren't that fun to operate. Pounding out a few blog posts per day was certainly not how I wanted to spend the rest of my life. I hired a couple of writers and set my personal finance websites on autopilot. They continued to do okay until 2011 when

Google started introducing significant changes into its search algorithm and have dwindled since then.

Fortunately, along the way, I had the insight to start building business with level-two characteristics. I had a few investing news websites, like American Banking and Market News, which got traffic from places like Stock Twits, Google Finance, MarketWatch and MSN Money. Eventually, I started collecting email addresses for my newsletter business that became ARN Daily and ARN Daily Premium.

In late 2012, I built another business called Lightning Releases that offers digital press release distribution to nonprofits, small businesses and authors. That business does not rely on any major platform for customer acquisition, makes use of my unique skills and abilities and has a growing list of customers and prospective customers.

This summer, I started yet another online business called GoGo Photo Contest, which allows humane societies and animal shelters to run photo contest fundraisers. All of our customers for that business come through email marketing and word of mouth. That business makes use of my unique skills and abilities and has a growing list of customers that could be leveraged in the future when we build out another web-based fundraising platform.

Final Thoughts

If you're going to build a business that's going to be successful over the long term, build something that not just anyone with some free time can build. Build a business that has some barriers to entry and makes use of your unique skills and abilities. Don't rely solely on traffic from Google or Facebook. Build a customer/subscriber list that you can leverage in the future. Build a level-two business.

7

Saying I Quit: Spring Cleaning in Business and in Life

As humans, we tend to get stuck in patterns and continue to do things simply because we've always done them, even if there's a better way to do something or it no longer serves a purpose. Every now and then, it's important to evaluate how you're spending your time and cut out things that once had a purpose, but no longer bring life to you so that you can focus on the things that matter the most.

In late 2012, I quit my day job so that I could spend more time with my premature, newborn son. (*That might sound like a crazy time to quit, but thankfully my business was already generating more income than my day job at that point*). Last summer, I decided to give up my adjunct teaching position at Dakota State University so that I could devote all my work effort to my business. Now that the snow is starting to melt, I've decided to do another round of spring cleaning in my business and in my life.

As an entrepreneur, I tend to come across more opportunities than most. If I see a business opportunity and believe I can capitalize on it, my natural inclination is to make it happen. Over a period of several years, I've ended up with a series of miscellaneous businesses and websites that generate a nominal percentage of my company's overall income (less than 10 percent), but take up a disproportionate amount of my time. So, I've decided to say "I quit" to these business units and only focus on the three business units that generate the vast majority of my company's revenue engine.

Effective today, I've shut down the marketing site for my website development business (Matthew Paulson Consulting) and will no longer be taking on new clients. I've come to realize that doing contract website development work for a variety of clients is less than an ideal business.

When you build a website for someone, you are generally only getting paid for your time and aren't building up a long-term income-generating asset. You also end up having to support all of the websites you had previously made for clients, which can be time consuming and unprofitable.

Consulting projects took up a significant portion of my time and mindshare in 2013, but only generated 5% of my company's total revenue. Therefore, I've decided to say goodbye to consulting in 2014.

I've also gone ahead and shut down a number of smaller online business ventures that I once thought to be significant opportunities but which I've let languish during the last few years. By eliminating these ancillary businesses, I'll be able to better focus on the three business units that generate the most revenue and have the best growth opportunities (Analyst Ratings Network, Lightning Releases and American Banking & Market News).

37signals recently underwent a similar re-evaluation, albeit at a much larger scale. They're divesting from all of their secondary products to focus solely on their flagship product, Basecamp. They're even changing the name of their company from 37signals to Basecamp. One of 37signals' values is to keep a small team (currently at about 43 employees) and they decided that it made more sense for them to focus on their one core business than to hire a bunch more people to work on their secondary products.

If you haven't re-evaluated how you spend your time lately, consider doing some spring cleaning so that you can focus on what matters to you the most. What has been taking up a disproportionate amount of time in your life that no longer serves its purpose? What parts of your work and life do you need to give up so that you can focus on what matters most to you?

8

My Gmail Productivity Hacks: Getting to Inbox Zero, Every Time.

One of the things that I've discovered about myself is that I do email very differently than most people. While I get anywhere from 75-150 new non-spam messages every day, my inbox regularly stays at a status of "inbox zero" (having no emails in my inbox). There are a few strategies that I make use of to do email effectively. If you plan on adopting these strategies, I first recommend declaring "email bankruptcy" and simply archiving all of the messages in your inbox. You'll get a fresh start at inbox zero and you'll likely hear back from anyone that you really needed to respond to anyway.

Here are the strategies that I use to hit inbox zero on a daily basis:

1. **Use a "Junk Mail" Label**

   Gmail provides a "report spam" button for any messages that come through that are genuine spam, but there are a lot of messages such as newsletters, messages from social media platforms and marketing emails that flood your inbox as well. I recommend creating a label called "Junk Mail" and creating filters for any sender that sends you email on your inbox that you really don't need to read (starting with messages from @twitter.com, @facebook.com and @linkedin.com) is a good start. I currently have more than 50 filters set to send specific types of messages to my junk mail folder. Every couple of days, I browse through the "Junk Mail" label and look for any important messages, then delete everything else in the label.

2. **Use Your Inbox as a To-Do List**

   Any message that stays in your inbox after an initial glance should be a message that you need to respond to within the next day. If you've read a message and don't need to respond to it, simply archive it. You can still search for it using Gmail's great search tools, but it won't be clogging up your inbox.

3. **Set Regular Email Checking Times**

   I think it's important to set specific times of day that you check your email. I generally do this during my least productive times of day, like when I get up in the morning and right after lunch. By setting 15 minutes (or so) aside to check and process your email, you're guaranteeing that you'll actually get to your email so that it won't pile up in your inbox.

4. **Turn off Inbox Tabs, Priority Inbox and Other Gimmicky Features**

Google regularly comes out with new features that help try to organize your inbox. I don't use any of them, because Google gets automatically labeling and filtering wrong more than it does right.

5. **Use Rapportive**

Rapportive is a great tool that will give you a good idea of who's emailing you. Rapportive will provide you links to social media profiles of anyone that's emailing you, as well as other pertinent contact information. It makes it easy to tell if someone that's sending you a message is someone you should be paying attention to.

6. **Combine Inboxes**

Before setting up my current email arrangement, I was checking four different accounts on a daily basis. I had two Hotmail accounts, a university account and an Outlook account for work. I used Gmail's "accounts" feature to suck all of my email into a single inbox for easier management.

7. **Don't Feel Obligated to Reply**

Unless someone is a family member or is paying you money, chances are you don't owe them anything. I get a lot of direct pitches from affiliate programs, display ad companies, recruiters, people looking to interview me and the like on a regular basis. Unless it's a particularly compelling pitch, I simply archive those messages and forget that I ever received them.

9

Will My Business Idea Make Any Money? Seven Questions to Ask…

If you want to start a business and have several ideas in mind, it's often hard to narrow down on a particular market you want to sell to. You might have several different competing ideas and aren't sure which one to focus on. You might not be sure which part of a market you want to tackle. You might suffer from a case of analysis paralysis and not make a decision about what kind of business you want to start, because you're afraid of making the wrong decision.

Fortunately, there are a few key questions that you can ask yourself that will help identify which of your business ideas you should pursue:

1. **Is there an existing market for my product/service?**
   If you're trying to build a new product or service that doesn't exist anywhere right now, you're going to face a very uphill battle because your customers don't even know that they need your product or service. If you're entering into an existing market that already has a lot of customers, you just need to create a product or service similar to what your competitors are selling and provide more value than they are or come up with a unique selling proposition (USP). If there are a lot of competitors in a market that means there are already a lot of companies making money in that market. Do not view having competitors in a market as a bad thing. That simply means the business model has already been proven.

2. **Do the skills my business requires line up with my strengths?**
   Make a list of the business skills that you're particularly good at and make a list of skills that your business will require to run successfully. There should be a strong correlation between those two lists. For example, my WordPress optimization service required an extensive knowledge of WordPress management, website performance and sales of digital products. I'm fairly good at all of those things, so it was a natural fit to set up that business. By starting a business that leverages your strengths, you'll avoid many of the mistakes you might make in businesses that you don't know as much about and don't have the particular skillset needed to run that business.

3. **Do I have a cost-effective way to reach my market?**
   If you build it, there's no guarantee that anyone's going to come. You need a reliable, repeatable way to reach your potential market of customers. Don't build your product or service and assume that you'll figure out how to market and sell it at a later date. Marketing is just as important, if not more important, than the actual development of your product or service. You need a way to easily identify and contact your potential customers affordably. This might be through direct mail, email marketing, targeted advertisements in trade magazines or pay-per-click advertising. Don't fool yourself by saying you're going to use search engine optimization (SEO) and social media to promote your product. Search engine optimization is not a long-term sustainable traffic strategy in most cases and it's very difficult to sell through social media. Find a way to directly identify and communicate with your target market.

4. **Can I offer a product or service my target market wants?**
   If you've identified a target market of customers that are already buying something, you need to determine whether or not you can realistically deliver on the product/service that they're already buying. If you can duplicate what your competitors are selling, then you simply need to find a way to offer more value than your competitors do or market your product/service better than they do. Even if your product is identical to your competitors' product, you can capture a chunk of the market by marketing your product/service better than they can.

5. Does my business wholly rely on someone else's ecosystem?

If your business is totally dependent upon Facebook, Google, Apple, Microsoft, eBay, Twitter or another NASDAQ-listed company to succeed, you're asking for trouble. Your business will only be successful as long as the company you're working through doesn't change the rules of the game. Consider how many eBay sellers were driven out of eBay's marketplace in the last several years because of changes to eBay's policies and fee structures. Think about how many companies were building the next great Twitter client, but were driven out of business when Twitter changed the rules of its APIs. It's okay to leverage social media platforms, app stores and search engines, but the majority of your business shouldn't rely on your company being in the good graces of any big technology company.

6. Can this business support the income that I want to make?

Some businesses have natural ceilings that are hard to get past. If you're looking to make $1 million per year, opening a small restaurant franchise like a smoothie shop or a Subway probably isn't the answer. With businesses like those, you end up making $50,000-$100,000 per year and end up working full time to get it. You need to make sure that your business can support the type of income that you're hoping to create. In order to figure this out, simply consider how many customers you can reasonably service and what each customer is worth to you per year.

7. What happens if I'm successful?

When setting up your business, you need to come up with a plan for success. What happens if demand for your business's product or service is much greater than you thought it would be? Would you be able to meet that demand? If your business is solely reliant on a particular skill that you use to offer a service or build a product, your business is going to hit a ceiling in revenue growth when you run out of time. When you're first starting up your business, you need to start thinking about how you're going to grow your business beyond yourself, what roles you might need to hire for, what equipment you might need, and generally, what your business looks like when it's much larger than it is now.

If you evaluate your list of business ideas against the seven questions above, you'll quickly end up with a much shorter list of ideas to choose from and hopefully be able to narrow it down to a single idea.

Also: I recently recorded a podcast episode on this topic with Peder Aadahl of the 168 Opportunities Podcast, titled Episode 062: Taking Your Gifts And Turning Them Into A Business With Matt Paulson.

10

Which is Riskier —
Getting a Job or Starting a Business?

Last week, I spoke about my business at Sioux Falls' 1 Million Cups Event. One of the questions I received was "What are the biggest existential threats to your business? In other words, what keeps you up at night?" My answer was, "Well, not much. I guess SendGrid could stop delivering my emails or Stripe could stop accepting credit cards on my behalf, but I think I could work around those issues." There appeared to be some in the room that were surprised by my answer. After all, isn't running a small business supposed to be risky?

Many people believe that there's a lot of risk in running a small business because of a frequently-cited SBA report that states half of small businesses fail within the first five years. Does this mean that everyone who's an entrepreneur that has a failed business loses a bunch of money and tucks their tail behind their legs and gets a job somewhere? Absolutely not. Often, when a small business "fails", it simply means that the entrepreneur has moved on to a better business. There are several businesses that I've started that have gone nowhere or have otherwise failed, but that doesn't mean that I'm a failure as an entrepreneur. I've simply moved on to building bigger and better businesses.

There's a lot less risk in small business than many realize. When I was working as a web developer at Factor 360, there was exactly one person (my boss) that could decide whether or not I could continue to work for his company. In business, it's considered risky to have the majority of one's work come from a single customer. Yet, as an employee, I only had one customer that was buying my services as a web developer and that's considered the "safe route." When you run a small business, you have dozens or even hundreds of people that have to decide to stop doing business with you before you quit making any money. I would much rather have the income that provides for my family come from 500 different customers paying me $10.00 a month than having one customer paying me $5,000.00 a month for my time.

When I had a day job, I had no managerial role in the company and really had no influence over several extremely important aspects of the company, including sales, marketing, project management, accounting, etc. Yet as an employee, I had to accept the economic consequences of the successes and failures of those components of the company. If the company wasn't doing enough in sales, I wouldn't (and didn't) get a raise. If there were no sales, I'd be out of a job as the result of someone else's failure in business. I would much rather be in a position where there are fewer parts of my business out of my control so that if I do fail, it's no one else's fault but mine.

One might argue that there's security in having a traditional job, but it's important to recognize that **everyone is self-employed.** You are responsible for providing employment (and an income) for yourself. If you were to quit showing up for work at your job, your customer (the company you work for) would stop paying you pretty quickly. As soon as you stop creating economic value for others, people will quit paying you, regardless of whether you're an employee or an entrepreneur.

The real way to find safety in your income is to provide the maximum amount of value to the maximum number of people. This happens best in running your own business where you have a lot of customers and you're highly motivated to succeed.

Go start your business. It's not as risky as you might think.

11

Want to Be a Millionaire? Become a Voracious Consumer of Content

Author Thomas Stanley did a survey of self-made millionaires and compiled the results in his best-selling book, *The Millionaire Next Door*. One of the interesting things that Stanley found in his survey results was that millionaires didn't tend to watch a lot of prime-time television, but they do read one nonfiction book per month on average. Will reading a nonfiction book every month make you a millionaire? I doubt it, but Stanley's research does illustrate the point that millionaires tend to be lifelong learners.

Self-made millionaires understand that there's a lot in the business world that they don't know. They recognize that the world is constantly changing and there's always new information to learn which could have a tangible impact upon their businesses. They know that there are critical pieces of information about their business and their industry that would be game-changing if they only knew them. The problem is, they don't yet know what they don't know. So, they embark on a journey of lifelong learning to become better entrepreneurs and more well-rounded people.

Lifelong learning can happen in any number of ways. You can read nonfiction books, but you can also listen to podcasts, read magazines, listen to audiobooks, audit university classes, watch documentaries and take online courses through places like Udemy or Coursera. Your learning style might not be ideally suited to reading a large number of books, but maybe you're an audio learner and would get a lot out of listening to podcasts and audiobooks. Maybe you're the type that learns by doing and would benefit from participating in workshops and hands-on classes. The key is to identify how you learn effectively and consume the mediums that you're best suited to.

I know that I don't have a very long attention span and can't read for hours at a time. But, I can read in 20 minute chunks and make sure that I read at least one chapter in whatever book I'm reading every morning. I know that I can listen to hours of podcasts on end and never really get tired of listening to them. I also do quite well in academic settings. In my journey of lifelong learning, I read anywhere from 50 to 75 books each year, listen to a couple dozen different podcasts each week and audit courses from local universities from time to time.

Most of the content you will consume won't lead to an immediate game-changing breakthrough in business, but every now and then, you'll find a needle in a haystack and uncover something that will change the way that you do business for the better. I can think of dozens of things that I've learned and implemented as a result of books that I've read, podcasts that I've listened to and online courses that I've taken.

If you'd like to have the same educational advantage that self-made millionaires do, the prescription is simple. Become a lifelong learner. Start reading at least one nonfiction book per month or engaging other relevant nonfiction content on a regular basis.

12

Please Don't Pitch Me on Your MLM

A couple of weeks ago, I started a new LinkedIn group for entrepreneurs in the Sioux Falls area. There was an individual that I was connected to on LinkedIn, but had never met in real life, that had joined the group. This person called me out-of-the blue one morning and asked if I was open to "new business opportunities." I said that I am.

This person immediately went into a script for a multi-level marketing company that sells anti-aging products and referred to it as an "exciting ground floor opportunity." I told this person that I generally don't accept solicitations regarding business opportunities unless they come from a trusted source. They responded along the lines of "Don't you know what a ground floor opportunity is?" I hung up on this person soon after.

I'm not writing this post to shame this individual. This is only an example of the many pitches I've received to become part of a multi-level marketing organization during the last several years. They almost always come from people that I barely know and pretend to be good friends with me when they make their pitch. I've always found these types of pitches offensive because I know that they really don't care about me and won't actually listen to anything I have to say.

Until recently, I haven't put a ton of thought into why pitches for multi-level marketing businesses are so offensive to me. If you take the time to think about what people who are pitching multi-level marketing companies are actually asking you to do, you'll realize how offensive those types of pitches actually are. While their pitch will likely be about a "ground floor" opportunity for you to "make a bunch of money," what they're really saying is this:

"I want you to come work for this company as an independent contractor selling products that you don't believe in so that I can make money off of your sales and referrals. Most people that partner with this company don't end up making any money, but if you do make money, it will be far less than you would be making at your job or in your business. Also, you'll be required to harass your friends and family members into becoming a distributor of products that you don't believe in as well, likely damaging those relationships in the process.

Oh, and you'll have to write a check for $250.00 for the opportunity to do so."

If you do want to pitch someone that you don't already know well on something, do it the right way. Try to have a mutual friend or business contact introduce you to the person that you want to pitch. Instead of finding someone's phone number and calling them out of the blue or pitching them at a party or another event, send them an email introducing yourself and ask if they'd be interested in a phone call or meeting about your opportunity. A pitch about a business opportunity should never be a surprise to the person receiving it. The pitch should just be one of many conversations you have with an individual if you're trying to get them to go into business with you. If the person you're pitching says they're firmly not interested, don't make a clandestine effort to overcome their objections. You're likely just going to make the person angry.

I won't go on about all of the problems with the multi-level marketing industry in detail, since it's already been done so well by others. If you want to work for a multi-level marketing company as an independent contractor and think that's your best opportunity, more power to you. Just leave me out of it.

13

Don't Become a Freelancer (Or, Why I'm Not Becoming a Commercial Drone Photographer)

A while back, I bought a DJI Phantom 2 Vision+ aerial drone and have taken some pretty cool pictures and video with it. Soon after I started posting my work, several people asked if they could pay me to take aerial photos of their businesses and property on their behalf. I also had several people suggest different ways that I might be able to monetize my hobby of aerial photography.

One person suggested I try doing some freelance work for a local news station. Another asked if I would do drone photography for their agency. Yet another suggested I try to do photography of school sporting events and try to sell pictures to parents.

Certainly someone could make money doing drone photography, if the FAA would stop dragging its heels on the issue. But, it's not going to be me. I really enjoy flying my drone and taking pictures with it, but I have zero interest in becoming a commercial aerial photographer. Despite having a really cool camera, I would still effectively be a freelance photographer. I have nothing against freelance photographers, but I wouldn't ever want to start a photography business or any business where I provide professional services on a freelance basis, such as graphic design, audio production or web development services.

What's wrong with freelancing?

1. **You stop getting paid when you stop working.**
   Professional photography is a classic example of a freelance services business. When you're a freelancer, you get paid a set fee for providing a specific service at a specific time, in this case, aerial photography. That means that you are only making money when you're working and actively providing services to customers. If you go on vacation or get sick, your business effectively grinds to a halt.

2. **You're effectively selling your time for money.**
   This is what you're doing when you have a full-time job. However, in this case, you have the additional administrative overhead of running a business and dozens of different bosses (your customers) to keep

happy. Depending on the type of freelance services you are offering, your schedule may be at the mercy of your customers because you need to be available when your customers aren't working.

3. **There's limited upside potential to your income.**
   If you were to charge $75.00 an hour providing some kind of freelance services and could book 30 hours of per week of billable work, the maximum that you could ever earn per year is about $115,000 (before expenses). While that's a nice income for an individual, it's not all that impressive of a business. In order to get beyond that cap, you would have to bring on team members to help perform your company's services or reduce your administrative overhead, which is feasible, but comes with another set of headaches.

4. **Freelance service businesses are difficult to sell.**
   Because so much of the business's value is tied up in the relationships that the owner has and the work performed by the owner. There's a good chance that your customers have a strong relationship with you and there's no guarantee that they are going to continue hiring whoever takes over your business. When these business do sell, they typically sell for relatively low revenue multiples.

What's the alternative?

I'm not opposed to the idea of a professional services business (such as photography). I just don't think you should be the person providing the service directly to your end customers. It might be a necessary evil to do the work yourself for the first couple of years, but your long term goal should be to have someone else or a series of systems and technology to provide the services on behalf of your company. When someone else is doing the work for your company, you are freed up to work on growing your business and tackling the tasks that only you as the business owner can tackle.

My investment newsletter business is an example of a services business done right. While it's a services business, I'm not directly responsible for providing the service (our daily newsletter) on a daily basis. The daily newsletter that customers pay for is delivered automatically through a series of software systems. Marketing effectively happens automatically through a series of campaigns that largely run themselves and customer service is primarily taken care of by my assistant. While I do have to intervene periodically, I'm largely free to focus my efforts on growing the business.

The other alternative is to build a product business, where you build something that customers can buy without you having to sell it directly. This can either be a consumer goods product, a piece of business equipment or even a digital product, like an e-book or an online course. You do the work to create the product once, then a series of systems sells and delivers the product on your behalf.

In both of these cases, there's an intentional disconnect between how the work is delivered to the end customer and the work that the owner does. As a business owner, your primary efforts must be focused on building and growing your business. That can't happen if you are directly responsible for producing the products or services that your customers purchase.

14

How Much Financial Runway Do You Have?

When you work for an employer, you know how much money you're going to earn in any month. You have a set salary or hourly rate and earn approximately the same amount of money each month. You also operate under the assumption that you're going to have the same job or a similar job indefinitely where you earn the same amount of money.

When you're an entrepreneur, these guarantees simply don't exist. Your income is irregular by nature and it can be very difficult to project how much income you're going to earn in the next several months.

You can't ever really know for sure if your business is going to keep generating about the same amount of money it currently is, whether or not you're going to see a significant jump in revenue or if your income is going to tank because of some future unknown event. You just don't know when a competitor is going to eat your lunch or when your business model is simply going to stop working.

For these reasons, it's especially important for entrepreneurs to keep track of some basic financial metrics so that you know how long you can weather the storm if you suddenly have a drop in income. The metric that best identifies how financially stable you are as an entrepreneur is your financial runway.

Financial runway is a measure of how many months you can go without earning any additional income before you run out of money.

Let's say that your business disappeared or you lost your job tomorrow and you have twelve months of expenses set aside. That means that you have one year to grow your business to the point where it generates enough income to provide for your monthly expenses before you run out of money. At the end of your one year financial runway, your business will either have taken off and will sustain your monthly living expenses, or you'll have crashed at the end of the runway and will have to go out and get a new job.

If you would like to know how much financial runway you have, I've set up a JavaScript calculator that you can use to calculate your runway. The calculator assumes that you're earning some amount of interest on your savings and investments and assumes that your expenses will increase by 3% per year because of inflation.

Access the Financial Runway Calculator at:

mattpaulson.com/2014/08/
how-much-financial-runway-do-you-have/

15

Marketing First: How to Avoid Having Zero Sales on Launch Day

I had the opportunity to chat with an entrepreneur who is building a mass-market physical product a few weeks back. We'll call him Fred for the sake of this discussion. Fred has been working on his project for over a year and has put the vast majority of his business effort into perfecting his product and the manufacturing process, but he hasn't done any work to generate interest in their product. Fred claims to have a marketing plan, but doesn't have a website, any sort of social media following or a list of people who have expressed any interest in the product.

Taking a Marketing Last Approach

Fred is making a mistake that many other first-time entrepreneurs have made. He's taking a "marketing last" approach. Like many other first time entrepreneurs, he thinks that marketing his product is something that will happen after he finishes developing his product or service. Some first-time entrepreneurs think that their product will be so good that they don't need to do any marketing. Others think that marketing isn't that big of a challenge and can be addressed by hiring an agency, setting up a Facebook page, or doing an advertising campaign. Fred is banking on the fact that specialty retailers will pick up his product and do the marketing for him. Fred doesn't realize that specialty retailers will probably be hesitant to pick up his product if no one's ever heard of it.

Unfortunately, Fred is probably in for a rude awakening when it comes time for his product to launch. Most people that don't get around to doing much marketing prior to launch end up having very lackluster sales (if any at all). People can't buy your product or service if they don't know about it. Unless you're executing a concerted marketing campaign prior to your launch, no one outside of your immediate circle of influence is going to have any idea that your product exists.

Even if you were to execute a great marketing plan a couple of weeks prior to your launch, you might not get any sales until several weeks later. It's very rare that people will purchase a product the first time they hear about it. It often takes several touch points to get a potential customer to the place where they will be willing to hand over their hard-earned cash for your product.

Of course, most marketing plans don't survive first contact with the customer. 75% of new marketing channels that you try either won't work or won't be a profitable way to attract new customers. If you plan on launching a product, but haven't done any pre-launch marketing, prepare to be disappointed on launch day. You will likely find yourself with zero sales and advertising initiatives that are barely paying for themselves.

Taking a Marketing First Approach

I recommend flipping the marketing and product development processes around. Before you even begin any serious product development, you should do these three things:

1. **Know Your Potential Customer.**

   Understand who your potential customers are. Are they male or female? How old are they? What are they interested in? Are they married? Do they have kids? Do they play any sports? How do they spend their free time? What common bonds tie your customers together?

2. **Talk To Potential Customers.**

   After you've identified the type of people you are targeting your product or service to, you should spend time talking to them about the problems they're facing and the category that your product is in. If you're building a better spatula, you would want to spend a lot of time talking to professional chefs about cooking equipment. What tools do they use that don't work as well as they should? What's slowing them down? In your conversations, you might find that they don't need a better spatula, but they do need a better blender. Talking to potential customers is the best way to reveal whether or not you are on the same page about your product.

3. Identify Marketing Channels.

After you have talked to some of your potential customers, you should have a list of 5-10 different ways that you will be able to reach your audience about your product. These could be things like advertising in a specific magazine, running a Google AdWords campaign or doing a direct mail campaign to a purchased list. Understand that most of the ideas that you come up with won't work, but a few of them will probably work quite well.

Once you've completed those tasks, you can begin working on your product. This doesn't mean you should forget about marketing and sales until launch day. While in your product development phase, you should be building an email list, a social media following and generating buzz about your product. You should also be researching and testing your potential marketing channel. There are probably other people that have launched products similar to yours. Find out how they market and sell their products. You should be putting 30-50% of your work effort into marketing and sales up to your product's launch date.

Realize that marketing and sales is a major part of getting your product or service off the ground. It's not an ancillary task that happens after your product is complete. Begin marketing before you start developing your product. Continue to market your product through the product development phase. Make your product launch a major event and continue to market your product in the weeks and months following the initial launch of your product.

16

Your Business Will Fail Eventually. Here's What To Do About It.

Ten years ago, you might have thought Blockbuster Entertainment was an unstoppable entertainment giant. The company had a near monopoly in the video and video game rental markets. At its peak in 2004, the company had 9,000 stores and 60,000 employees. Just six years later, the company went bankrupt. Blockbuster simply couldn't compete with its cheaper and more convenient competitors (Netflix, Amazon and Redbox).

The market had fundamentally changed and Blockbuster was not able to adapt quickly enough to the new reality of how movies are being rented. The business model of going to a physical store to rent VHS/DVD movies that took off in the 1980's simply no longer worked. The idea came and went.

The Business Category Lifecycle

Every category of business has a natural lifecycle. New businesses, products, inventions come along and push aside what came before them. The movie rental store industry was a 30 year idea (1980-2010) only to be replaced by online rentals. Dial-up internet was popularized in the 1990's, only to be replaced a decade later by high-speed internet services. Land-line phones became widespread in the early 1900's and were largely replaced just over a century later by cellphones. At some point, just about every type of product or service will be supplanted by something new. Even paper books that have been dominant for the last 600 years are beginning to be replaced by an electronic equivalent.

Often, the companies that were previously dominant (like Blockbuster) aren't able to adapt to new realities of business. They cling to the business models that served them well for many years. They are surpassed by new companies that champion new product categories and new types of services.

We see this with cable companies today. Consumers want always-available on-demand content served through the web from companies like Netflix, Hulu Plus, Amazon and Aereo, but cable companies are addicted to the revenue from monthly cable subscriptions and aren't willing to provide consumers what they actually want.

As a result, consumers are quickly cutting their cable and moving to more consumer-friendly online services. I would be surprised if cable companies still exist in their current form 15 years from now.

Planning for Disruption

As an entrepreneur, it's scary to think the economics of the industry you're in may fundamentally change. The cash cow that you've had for years might be replaced by an upstart competitor that offers something quicker, cheaper and more effective.

Unfortunately, we don't know ahead of time if our business ideas are a 2-year idea, a 5-year idea, or a 50-year idea. We do know that at some point the natural life cycle of our businesses are going to come to an end. At some point, your business will fail. You can only hope that your business will continue to exist until the point that your industry is disrupted by some outside force, whether that be macro-economic forces, new competitors, new product categories or some other unknown black swan event. It's a matter of when, not if.

It would be a lot easier if we knew in advance when our businesses would no longer be economically viable. We could plan ahead and start something new well in advance of when our businesses are going to get disrupted by something else. Since we can't predict the future, we should plan assuming that our business may no longer exist in the near future. There are two ways to do this: get your finances in order and adopt a portfolio model of doing business.

By having a solid financial life, you'll be able to personally weather a decline in income in the event that your business fails for whatever reason. I don't have any special advice that Dave Ramsey, Clark Howard or Suze Orman wouldn't offer. Reduce the amount of debt that you have, build a sizable emergency fund, live within your means, save for retirement and for your kids' college. If you're looking for a plan to follow, check out Dave Ramsey's baby steps.

The Portfolio Model of Entrepreneurship

Adopting a portfolio model of business is a more complicated matter. A portfolio entrepreneur operates multiple businesses in different industries knowing that the income their businesses generate may ebb and flow over time. As one business grows, another might decline. By having a few different businesses, your income is more insulated in the event that one of your business fails. For example, I publish an investment newsletter, offer fundraising software to animal shelters and humane societies and operate a press release distribution business. If the stock market were to take a significant nosedive and my investment newsletter was no longer a viable business, I would still be able to rely on the income from my other two businesses while I work to replace the business that failed.

Don't get me wrong. I'm not saying you should try to build three businesses at once. That doesn't work. You should work on one business until it becomes self-sustainable and doesn't require your day-to-day attention. At that point, you should look to diversify and try to build another income stream in a different category.

Buckle Your Seatbelt

Whether you're an entrepreneur or an employee, it's very likely the business that you're involved with ten or twenty years from now won't be the same business you're involved in today. We shouldn't be surprised when some outside force causes us to make a job or a business transition. It's going to happen sometime, so be prepared for it.

17

Entrepreneurship is an Endurance Sport

If you have never built a successful business, you might think the dream of building a profitable company is something that you won't ever be able to achieve. If you've tried to start a business that didn't work out, you might think you just don't have what it takes to build a profitable business. You might look at a successful entrepreneur and think that they can be successful at anything they put their mind to. They have the Midas touch and don't have to deal with failure, right?

Successful entrepreneurs usually have several failed businesses on their resume, but they rarely talk about or get asked about their past failures. It's easy to think that they've never failed at anything, but every entrepreneur that has been in business for any length of time will face some form of failure. You are going to face failure at some point or another as an entrepreneur, it's just a matter of how you're going to react to that failure. You can admit defeat and give up your dream of owning your own company. Or, you can try to understand what caused you to fail and then get back up and try again. In order to succeed over the long term, you have to have the endurance to push through and keep trying even after a major setback or the total failure of your current business.

An Overnight Success, 7 Years Later...

It's easy to look at the success that someone like me has had and think "I could never get there." While I run a handful of highly profitable companies now, you didn't see me in 2006, 2007 and 2008 when I was first trying to build an internet business. I tried to create a bunch of different websites and online businesses that just never got any traction. I tried to create an audiobook recommendation website that failed to get any attention. I tried to create a podcast directory that I never even finished building. I tried to create a network of personal finance blogs that had some success, but failed following a series of changes to Google's ranking algorithms. Eventually, I tried enough things that I had a decent idea of what would work and what wouldn't work and was able to build a profitable business based on my experience.

It wasn't until 2010 that my company generated enough revenue to provide me a salary similar to what I had been making at my day job. It took another full three years before people really started to take notice of the success I was having with my business. Now, seven years into the process, I'm finally an "overnight success."

Success Follows Failure

Your first real entrepreneurial success will likely come after a series of failures. When you're first getting started building a business, you are going to have absolutely no idea what you're doing (and that's okay). Your first business will probably fail. Your second business might fail a little bit less. By the time you're on your third business, you might catch onto something that actually works. After you've been in business long enough, you will have identified a lot of things that don't work and a handful of strategies that do work to build a successful business. Eventually, you'll have a decent idea of what it actually takes to get a profitable company off the ground.

It takes a while to become successful in business. Entrepreneurship is a marathon. Becoming a successful entrepreneur and building a profitable company will require working on your business full time over the course of several years. Malcolm Gladwell's 10,000 hour rule is in full effect. In order to really know what you're doing, you need to work on your business for 10,000 hours. That's working on your business full-time for five years. Don't think that you can work on a business for a couple of months, take a break from it, and think you've really gotten anywhere.

18

How to Recognize and Attract New Business Opportunities

When people ask about the various businesses that I run, one of the most common follow-up questions that I receive is "What's next for you? What's the next business that you're going to start?" As someone that runs a few different profitable online businesses, it would be natural to think that I have a list of the next 5 to 10 business ideas I want to pursue in a Word document somewhere and will be pursuing those ideas as soon as I have enough time to do so. However, that's not the case.

I actually have no idea what my next business venture will be and I'm really not all that worried about it. Instead of strategizing about the next several businesses I'm going to start, I simply wait for the right opportunity to knock on my door and pursue it to the best of my ability.

American Consumer News, LLC in 2010 vs. 2014

Four years ago, my company looked completely different than it does today. At the time, my business consisted of four different personal finance blogs which made money primarily from contextual advertising (Google AdSense) and sponsored blog posts. My business was going after a very different target market and made a fraction of the revenue that it does today. Quite frankly, the business model I was using at the time wouldn't work today and that's okay. At the time, I didn't have a grand vision for the series of online businesses that I run today, which begs the question of how these businesses came to be if I didn't have a master plan for the direction of my company.

The reality is that I have exactly one strategy for building new businesses. I wait for opportunity to show up, and pursue it to the best of my ability.

In 2010, I saw that the content I was publishing about investing was getting a lot of traction through places like Google Finance, Twitter and StockTwits. I saw that it was a major opportunity to build an audience of investors and realized that if I was able to publish substantially more content than I was at the time, I would be able to reap a substantial amount of advertising revenue. I seized the opportunity and built out software systems and brought on team members to maximize that opportunity.

Four years later, my network of financial news websites is garnering approximately 2.5 million page views per month.

The same could be said about my other two businesses. I started Lightning Releases after recognizing that I could build a competitive news distribution network and could market a press release distribution service relatively cheaply and effectively. I co-founded GoGo Photo Contest after I was approached by a friend that wanted to start the business but didn't have the business building or marketing expertise that I had. I decided to write a book after recognizing that my good friend Andy Traub could help set up boundaries and a system to ensure that I actually finish the project.

Identifying Real Business Opportunities

If you are or want to become an entrepreneur, opportunities will knock on your door. These opportunities could be people that want to do business with you, a new potential market that you identify, a business deal that could potentially grow your business, a customer that wants you to develop a new product or service or even someone that wants to hire you for a job. Some of them you will be able to immediately discount, like multi-level marketing companies disguised as "ground floor" opportunities. Some opportunities will be a very easy yes and other opportunities won't be so clear.

If we had the foresight to see what the results of pursuing every potential business opportunity would be five years down the road, there would be a lot more people willing to do the work of becoming an entrepreneur.

Unfortunately, we don't know what we don't know. We simply have to evaluate each opportunity based on the information available and make a best guess as to whether or not it's something we should pursue.

Here are some questions you should ask yourself about every potential business opportunity you could pursue:

- Who is the person presenting this opportunity? How well do I know them? What kind of track record do they have?

- Do I have the expertise necessary to pursue and maximize this opportunity? If not, am I able to leverage someone else's talent to leverage this opportunity?

- How much work will I need to put in to seize and maximize the results of pursuing this potential opportunity?

- If everything goes as planned, what's the most amount of money I will be able to make by pursuing this opportunity?

- If I pursue this opportunity, what won't I be able to do? What trade-offs will there be?

- How interested am I in this opportunity? Do I want to pursue it? (If your answer isn't a "heck yes," say no.)

But Opportunities Aren't Knocking On My Door...

If you are not regularly running into job and business opportunities, there's a strong likelihood that you simply don't know enough people. Ideally, you should have as many as 100 loose business acquaintances in the same or similar industries as you that you touch base with every few months. I've found that it's relatively easy to make new business contacts by attending events relevant to my business and by inviting people out to lunch on a regular basis. I've taken the advice of *Never Eat Alone* by Keith Ferrazzi quite seriously and buy people lunch in my community at least three days each week. I've made dozens of new business contacts as a result of simply asking "Hey, would you be interested in grabbing lunch sometime?" on a regular basis.

The other way to recognize business opportunities is to become a voracious learner. If you commit to being a lifelong learner and regularly learn new things about your industry and business in general, you'll begin to recognize business opportunities—whether that be potential ways to grow your existing business or a potential new business that you could start.

Wait for the Right Opportunity. Seize it. Maximize it.

You really don't need a grand vision for what your business looks like five years down the road. Instead, you just need to put yourself out there and continually learn about your industry and business in general. New business opportunities will start popping up. You will need wisdom and discernment to evaluate whether or not an opportunity is worth pursuing. Finally, you'll need real ambition to pursue and maximize an opportunity when a true business opportunity surfaces.

19

How to Add Rocket Fuel to Your Product Launch with a Podcast Tour

When most people release a book with a traditional publisher, they will make a series of appearances at local bookstores as part of their marketing strategy—commonly known as a book tour. Since my book was being published exclusively through Amazon, it only made sense to do a virtual book tour.

Instead of reaching potential readers in person a few hundred people at a time by being the guest of a local bookstore, I would attempt to reach a few thousand potential readers at a time by being a guest on a variety of business and entrepreneurship podcasts. Since the type of readers I was targeting listened to shows like Entrepreneur On Fire, Internet Business Mastery and TropicalMBA, it was a no-brainer to try to get in front of their audiences as part of the marketing strategy for my book launch.

Identifying Podcasts to Target

The first step of the process was to identify the shows that I wanted to pitch myself to be a guest on. I started with the list of business podcasts that I listen to on a weekly basis, then added a number of shows that I know some of my contemporaries have been interviewed on. I also looked on iTunes' business sections to see which podcasts were most downloaded. My book coach also suggested a few shows to target.

I ended up with about 40 podcasts that I could potentially target. In order to pare this number down, I went through and removed the shows that don't normally have guests on them and listened to the others to see if the content of my book would be a good fit for their audiences. I was hoping to get onto 10 to 15 podcasts, so I cut the total number of people I planned on pitching down to 25 knowing that they wouldn't all say yes.

Making the Pitch

Whenever you're making a pitch on anything, the worst thing you can do is make it all about you. Nobody wants to hear a pitch that's only about how they can help you. I was very careful to avoid that mistake as part of the pitch email that I used. Instead, I tried to focus on the value that I could bring to them and their audience. My book coach and I collaborated on two different pitch emails, one for people that I don't know and one for people that I have a pre-existing relationship with.

Here's the template email I used to pitch the podcast hosts that I didn't have a personal relationship with. I customized each message for each recipient, but the text below is pretty close to what they received.

NAME,

Your time is valuable so I'll keep my email brief.

Frankly, until now you've done a lot more work helping business owners than I have.

If you think it would help your audience, I'd like to share some of the lessons I've learned along the way to building my own seven figure business. (You can read my bio at: http://www.mattpaulson.com/about/ if you'd like.)

In late July I'm releasing my first book, "40 Rules for Internet Business Success: Learn How to Escape the 9 to 5, Do Work that You Love and Build a Profitable Online Business."

Just pick a topic or topics that you think your audience would benefit from and we can formulate a plan to share it with them.

[list of 40 rules]

Thanks for being awesome,

Matthew Paulson

Preparation and Interviewing

Sending out the initial ask was the easy part. Out of the 25 podcasts hosts that I pitched, 12 of them said yes. Most of the rejections were polite "no's" and a few didn't respond. It would be very easy to take this personally and take each "no" as a personal rejection, but it's important to remember that your agenda and everyone else's agendas are never going to perfectly align. You can't expect everyone to put their agenda aside for yours just because you want them to. Several of the "no's" were kind enough to tweet about my book on launch day and a few of them even mentioned the book on their shows.

Of the 12 podcast hosts that said yes, I asked each one what direction they wanted to go with the podcast and asked if they would send a list of questions ahead of time to help me prepare. Some were organized and had their entire list of questions ready a week ahead of time, while others were very much off the cuff. I tried to accommodate each host's schedule as best as I could.

I ended up recording all 12 interviews in a period of about two weeks. Each interview took about an hour of preparation and another hour of actually doing the interview, not to mention the time emailing back and forth with the hosts of the shows I was going to be on. When all was said and done, I spent a better part of a week preparing for and recording the interviews. It felt like a lot of work.

The Results

As of October 1st, I sold about 750 copies of my book. It's hard to attribute a specific percentage of those sales to the podcast tour, but I did see significant bumps in sales of the book on the days when the podcast episodes came out. If I had to guess,

I would attribute about 40% of those sales directly to being a guest on other people's podcasts. Since new podcast listeners will often go back and listen to back episodes of shows, people will be hearing about my book for the first time for months and years to come.

As I've previously mentioned, one of the best parts about writing a book is the indirect benefits. I met a lot of cool people over Skype during the podcast tour, including Chris Locurto, Spencer Hawes, Chris Guthrie, John McIntyre and Terry Lin to name a few. I even plan on meeting up with a few of them later this month in Las Vegas at a conference called Rhodium Weekend.

The Podcast Tour Strategy

While I conducted a podcast tour for the launch of my book, I think this strategy can be effectively used as part of the launch of a wide variety of products. If you are making something that someone else's audience is interested in, you have a legitimate shot at getting on relevant podcasts. You shouldn't expect that the entire podcast will be about your product, because nobody likes a pitch fest. However, if you can provide educational and entertainment value to listeners of someone else's podcast, they will probably want to hear from you again and will subscribe to your email list or purchase your product.

20

Let's Get Better at Saying "No!"

During the last few years, I've built up a wide network of loose business connections in Sioux Falls and around the world by attending events, buying people lunch, and simply being engaged in business and an active member in the community. Because I'm a person that's more "out there" than most, there's not a week that goes by where I don't get pitched on something.

Typically a well-intentioned individual will want me to set up some sort of business partnership with them or want me to help out with or give money to their non-profit organization or want me to coach them in business. These requests range from simple "Can I pick your brain?" requests all the way up to, "Hey, we should start a business together."

What Happens When You Say "Yes" Too Often

For a while, I tried to accommodate all of the requests that I could reasonably accommodate because I wanted to help people out and I wanted other people to like me. I ended up having a lot of "irons in the fire" and I wasn't all that excited about many of them. I had gotten myself into a couple of business relationships I wasn't all that excited about and was giving money to a couple of non-profit organizations that I wasn't really emotionally invested into.

I simply tried to do too many things at once. I thought I was helping people by saying "Yes" to everybody, but I was really doing them a disservice because I wasn't doing anything well. I was doing a lot of things poorly. I had no margin in my life and areas of my life that should be important were taking a backseat to less important things.

Identify and Focus on Critically Important Areas of Life

Eventually, I figured out that I have a limited amount of time, energy and money and need to allocate those resources very intentionally. A lot of people will say that time is the most limited resource that you have, because you only get 168 hours each week. The reality is that it's even more precious than that.

How many productive mental hours do you have in a day, really? If you're lucky, you have 30-35 good hours of productive mental energy in the week. After a certain point in the day, you might still be at work, but your brain isn't in a place where you can actually get anything meaningful done.

I know that I have the time, energy and financial resources to do a handful of things very well and need to say "no" to everything that doesn't fit within the narrow band of things that I consider very important.

These are the only things that I say "Yes" to consistently:

- Maintaining my mind, body and soul (lifelong learning, physical exercise, personal faith and prayer)
- Spending time with my wife and son
- Building technology-driven systems-based businesses with trusted business partners
- Maintaining healthy relationships with friends and acquaintances
- Supporting Christian ministries (that I'm passionate about) with my time and money

If something doesn't fall into one of those five categories, the overwhelming likelihood is that I'll say no. If I want to make those five areas of my life a priority and do them well, I have to intentionally say "No" to everything else.

I suggest that you identify the four or five areas of your life that are especially important to you and focus on them. Use those areas of critical importance as a filter. If something doesn't fall into one of those areas, don't commit to it.

Reasons to Say No

If you aren't sure whether or not you should say "Yes" or "No" to something, here are a few good questions you should ask yourself:

- How excited am I about this opportunity? You should only say "Yes" to things that you are excited about and can't help but say "Yes" to. If you're not absolutely sure you want to do something, let the answer be "No."

- Do I trust the person making the request? This is especially important when considering business partnerships and requests for charitable donations. I will automatically say "No" to most business partnerships unless I have a pre-existing relationship with the person making the request.

- Do I know what I'm signing up for? If I say "Yes", how much time will be required of me? What kind of work will I be signing up for? How long am I committing my time for? I won't say "Yes" to something until I know precisely what the commitment will be.

- Does this further an area of critical importance in my life? Does saying "Yes" to this further any of the areas of critical importance I've identified? If it doesn't, you probably shouldn't say "Yes."

- Is this the best opportunity I have available? Because you only have so much useful mental energy in a day, you should only do the things that will have the greatest impact on your areas of critical importance.

- Would I be saying "Yes" just to make the person that asked happy? Don't spend your life being a people pleaser. You'll just end up miserable.

Do More by Doing Less

The true key to productivity, work-life balance and dare I say, happiness, is to identify the few areas of life that are especially important to you and giving a resounding "no" to everything else.

21

The Value of a "Million Dollar Idea"

When I was eleven years old, I spent a lot of time playing Sim City 2000 and its sister games, such as SimTower, SimCopter and SimEarth. I even made a website called "SimWeb" hosted on GeoCities that had cheat codes, saved games and demo downloads for my favorite games.

One day, I had the idea that it would be really cool for Maxis (the maker of SimCity) to build a game called SimHuman that allowed you to live the life of a person, build a house, have a job, etc. I thought it was such a good idea, that I even emailed the game idea to Maxis.

Five years later, Maxis and Electronic Arts launched The Sims franchise and went on to sell 175 million copies. I had the same great idea that the game designers at Maxis had. They made billions of dollars in revenue from one of the most successful game franchises in history and I made nothing. The difference between Maxis and eleven-year old Matthew Paulson? Maxis executed on the idea and turned it into reality.

This story illustrates a lesson that every entrepreneur should understand: **A million dollar idea is worth zero dollars until it actually gets implemented.**

The Value of an Idea

A lot of people believe they have the next million dollar product idea. They think that if they could just get their idea in front of the right person, they would be set for life. Someone else would do all of the work and they would get big royalty checks for being the person that came up with the idea. Unfortunately, that almost never happens. Unless you are able to develop a truly remarkable business or product idea, get it patented and find a company that wants to execute on your idea, it's extremely unlikely that anyone is going to pay you for your idea.

Companies are hesitant to pay anyone for ideas because ideas in and of themselves do not generate any economic value (even good ideas). Economic value is only created when someone takes an idea and implements it in such a way that other people find valuable enough to pay for it. Think you've come up with an idea for a better mousetrap? Your neighbor with mice in his or her basement probably isn't going to pay you for the idea, but he or she might pay you for the actual mousetraps after you've proven out your idea and manufactured them.

What To Do With Your Million Dollar Idea

If you believe you have a million dollar idea for a product or service, holding onto it tightly and looking for someone else to turn your idea into reality is not the answer. Instead, take your business or product idea and try to turn it into reality yourself. If it really is a million dollar business or product idea, you will make a million dollars when you turn it into a successful business. If it doesn't work… well, then it wasn't really a million dollar idea, was it?

22

I Build Digital Vending Machines for a Living

Whenever someone asks me what I do for a living, I have a hard time explaining that I publish an investment newsletter, operate a press release writing and distribution business, offer a service to help animal shelters to raise money and build educational training products for golfers. The various businesses that I'm involved in have almost nothing to do with each other in terms of audience and interest, but they all effectively follow the same business model. I've recently thought of a new way to communicate the types of businesses that I run and I thought I would share it with you today.

I Build Digital Vending Machines for a Living

Consider how a vending machine transaction works:

- A customer walks up to the vending machine and the vending machine has something that the customer wants (usually pop or candy).

- The customer puts money into the vending machine via cash or credit card.

- The vending machine drops the item the customer purchased into a slot and the customer takes their item and walks away satisfied.

- Every few weeks, an employee of the vending machine company checks in on the vending machine, refills the inventory and picks up the cash.

Customers can become aware of a vending machine, identify that the vending machine has something they want and complete the transaction without a human ever being involved. Certainly there's some up-front work for the entrepreneur that sets up the vending machine. They have to find a good location, negotiate a deal with the owner of the location, purchase the equipment, place the vending machine and stock it with candy or pop. After the vending machine is set up, the business effectively runs itself.

The Anatomy of a Digital Vending Machine

Effectively, I've replicated this business model using the internet. I will do a lot of up-front work to identify a market need, build out a digital product or service, create an automated sales funnel to acquire new customers and set up an automated checkout and delivery system. After the product or service launches, the business will effectively run itself since all of the customer touch points happen using software and automated processes.

Here is the basic business model that I use for my companies:

- A customer will become aware of the company by way of advertising, search engine optimization, email marketing or social media.

- The customer will provide their email address to receive some sort of lead magnet, such as a free guide or newsletter.

- The customer will receive a series of emails (an autoresponder series) that contains tips and information about the company's products and services.

- The customer will decide that they want to buy the digital product or service and will click through to a sales page.

- The customer will provide their payment information into the order form and the product or service will be delivered to them automatically using software.

- Every week, I receive a payment from our payment provider (Stripe) for the previous week's purchases.

Effectively, a customer can become aware of one of my products or services, decide that they want to order it, place their order and receive said product or service without me ever being involved. After a digital vending machine is set up, I just need to check on it periodically to make sure everything is running smoothly. I can also spend some time working to improve said product or service, but I don't have to if I don't want to.

The Ultimate Lifestyle Business

Running a "digital vending machine" business has a lot of nice benefits. First, you literally make money while you sleep. It's pretty fun to wake up in the morning and see that I made a few hundred dollars overnight. Second, when you're not actively working on building a new "digital vending machine" (a new business) or working to improve one of your existing products or services, there's really not that much work to do. Finally, you have a lot of flexibility about when and where you work. If my family wants to take an 8 or 9 day vacation, it's not that big of a deal because I can make sure I'm not working on any new projects during that time and effectively put my business on autopilot. I will typically work about an hour a day while on vacation to keep email manageable.

There you have it. I build digital vending machines for a living.

23

Why You Should Say No to Side Projects

A couple of weeks back, I had the opportunity to travel to Las Vegas for an event called Rhodium Weekend. I wasn't entirely sure what to expect going into the event, but there were a lot of people that I knew online who would be attending the event that I was looking forward to meeting in person, like Justin Cooke and Joe Magnotti, Chris Guthrie, Spencer Hawes and several others. The primary focus of the event was buying and selling income-generating websites, but I came out of the conference with a very different take-away regarding the future direction of my business.

The Power of Focus

One of the consistent themes that came up over and over again during the conference was focus. After you reach a certain point of success, it doesn't make sense to keep working on smaller side projects that you set up years ago when you were first getting started.

In other words, why would you put any effort into thinking about a website that generates $100 per month when you have another website that generates $5,000 per month? You only have so much emotional and mental energy to commit toward work and other projects. Having too many irons in the fire creates distraction and prevents you from working on what's most important to you.

Two entrepreneurs at the event shared how they had recently jettisoned all of their side projects to focus exclusively on their core business. They had started trying out different online businesses beginning in 2010, but it wasn't until last year that they came across a business venture that really took off in a serious way.

Their new business quickly became responsible for the vast majority of their company's revenue, but all of the business projects they had built in the past were still taking up quite a bit of their time. These businesses generated a serious amount of revenue, but took up a disproportionate amount of time for the amount of income that they generated.

They did something pretty bold that has really made me do a lot of thinking. They sold off, shut down or gave away all of their secondary businesses to focus exclusively on growing their primary business unit. In doing so, they jettisoned approximately $20,000 in monthly revenue and $5,000 in monthly profit. The move was financially painful initially, but the move allowed them to reach a new level of business success because they weren't focusing their mental energy on their side projects.

My Take-Away and Action Plan

I've been building online businesses since late 2006. For the first five years, I tried to create a wide variety of different online businesses and income generating websites. Many of them were miserable failures and a few had moderate success. In 2010, I started my financial news business, Analyst Ratings Network, which has become responsible for 80% of the revenue that my company makes on a monthly basis. However, I still spend a lot of time working to maintain the other business ventures that I've started during the last several years at the expense of working on Analyst Ratings Network.

For this reason, I plan to significantly reduce the number of secondary projects that I'm working on over the next 12 months. Earlier this year, I made a few changes to reduce my ongoing commitments. Now, I'm going to take it to the next level. I'm going to sell, give away or shut-down about ten smaller websites that I've been running for the last several years.

I've already taken action on four of them over the weekend. I plan to further reduce the amount of consulting I do by transitioning most (if not all) of my remaining consulting clients to an agency that can take better care of them. I may sell my press release writing and distribution business, which is responsible for about 10% of my company's monthly revenue, if I find the right buyer. Finally, I'm going to commit to not starting any new projects in 2015. That will allow me to focus almost exclusively on Analyst Ratings Network. I will continue to be involved in GoGo Photo Contest and USGolfTV as well, although I have pretty limited roles with both companies.

What Do You Need to Cut Out?

We're all involved in things that we probably shouldn't be. At a point in the past, you signed up for something that you thought was a good idea at the time. It could be a volunteer position or group that you're a part of. It could be a business venture or a part-time job. It could be a hobby or some other on-going commitment. The only reason that you're still doing it is because you made a decision several months or years back that it was a good idea. You would never sign up for it again today, but haven't stopped doing whatever it is because you perceive that the pain of maintaining the status quo is less than the pain of making a change.

What do you need to give-up in 2015 and beyond?

24

How to Fail Miserably When Pitching Someone

I've made it a point to get better connected to the entrepreneurial community in the city I live in within the last year (Sioux Falls, SD). I've been going to a lot more events, have sponsored a few different things and have made some great connections by buying people lunch. As a natural consequence, my name has become more known in this community and I've had a number of people reach out to me.

How to Fail Miserably When Pitching Someone

Most have been well meaning and simply wanted to ask questions about business and I've done my best to accommodate them. There have been a couple of exceptions though. There have been a couple of people that have asked to meet with me under questionable pretenses, saying that they wanted to chat about entrepreneurship and building businesses. In reality, they either wanted to try to sell me on something directly or have me promote whatever they're selling for them.

Here's an example of one of these emails:

"First of all I want so say kudos for being involved in as many areas of the community as you are. Just reading up on all of the organizations you are a part of or help out has me exhausted ha! I am a Financial Advisor with [NAME OF COMPANY] and am extremely intrigued by some of the work you are doing. My main focus is more on long term financial planning and security, so maybe a tad different from what you typically analyze. I would love to grab coffee with you to sit down and see if I could potentially be a resource for some of the entrepreneurs you work with on a regular basis?"

My initial thought after reading this email was "Wow. That sounds like a great deal for you." If you're trying to set up a meeting with someone you've never met, you need to give them a good reason to actually meet with you. If you're asking for a meeting with someone you've never met before that can help you in business, chances are that their time is pretty valuable. You can't expect anyone is going to want to give you any of their time just because you want to sell them on something or you think that they can help you with your business.

How to Pitch the Right Way

You need to find a way to provide them value up-front so that the person actually wants to meet with you. Try to find a way to provide value or insight into their business. Maybe you know something about business that would help the person you're trying to meet with. Maybe you and the other person share a mutual interest that you could have a conversation about over lunch or coffee. The key is to show the other person that you have something to contribute to the conversation.

If you do want to pitch somebody you don't know on something, you need to build a bit of a relationship before pitching them. Try to create a series of personal "touch points" with the person through attending events, social media and casual conversation (whether that be in-person or online). I would be much more open to hearing from someone that wanted to pitch me on something if I had a brief conversation with them at a 1 Million Cups event or if they've left a couple of insightful comments on my blog. That shows that you've put at least some effort into getting to know them before pitching them.

Here's an example of an email I might send to someone that I want to meet with.

Dear Andy –

My name is Matthew Paulson. I recently read your book "The Early to Rise Experience". In the book, I see that you recommend turning off the television 2 hours before bed to sleep better. Did you know that X, Y and Z also have a significant impact on your ability to get a good night's sleep? I've personally had good luck with A, B and C and now can regularly get up at 5:00 AM without an alarm clock.

Anyway, I'll be in your town in a couple of weeks. If you have an hour, I'd love to get together for lunch or coffee to connect and chat about business.

Let me know.

Thanks!

Matt

25

The Best Way to Make More Money is...

Every January, I help coordinate a Financial Peace University class at my church. The class shows people how to create a budget, get out of debt, set up proper insurance, plan for retirement and make other important financial decisions. All of the teaching in the class is about how to better spend money you already have, but sometimes the problem is that you're simply not making enough money to get by.

If you have a couple of kids and only make $12.00 an hour at a retail or service job, it's going to be very difficult to get ahead by only changing what you do with your current income. Sometimes you just need to make more money. If you can't achieve your current financial goals with the income that you have now, you'll need to find a way to make more money. Granted, saying that you need to make more money and actually finding a way to make more money are two entirely different things.

The best way to make more money is to do more of what you're already doing.

A while back, I was doing a coaching call with a guy that helps people set up email marketing campaigns. He was making about $5,000 a month at the time and wanted to double his income. He was considering offering additional services, going into a different business and trying a lot of other things that he wasn't an expert at. All of the ideas that he had involved starting over with something new to create an additional income stream. While it can be alluring and fun to try to start something new from scratch, usually the easiest way to make more money is to do more of what you're already doing. My advice to him was to keep doing what he was doing, but find a way to service twice as many customers as he's currently serving. He would need to ramp up his marketing efforts and bring on an additional person to help do the work, but following those steps is a much clearer route to creating additional income than trying to start something brand new from scratch.

It's much easier to grow what's already working than to try to create something new from scratch. In other words, going from one customer to five customers is much easier than going from zero customers to one customer. If you've already proven out an idea, simply repeating the process with another customer is a lot easier than trying to prove out an entirely new idea.

How to Do More of What You're Already Doing

If you're an entrepreneur, the path to doing more of what you're already doing is much clearer. You find the systems and the people you need in order to ramp up your production capacity and work on developing new marketing channels to get additional customers. It would be nice if there was a magical formula to double your sales and your operational capacity, but there just isn't. You just need to try new ways to market your business until you find something that works and scale up your operational capacity accordingly.

If you have a day job and are working for someone else, the path to do more of what you're already doing is less clear. It's still very doable though. Your employer has hired you because you provide some specific value to the company that's worth more than the money they're paying you. Identify what special skills and talents that you bring to the table that create value for your company. If you have a specific professional skill like graphic design, programming, accounting, law, sales or marketing, it's very easy to identify how you create value for your company. If it's not entirely clear what your unique ability is, try to identify what problems you solve for your employer or what need lead them to hire you in the first place.

Once you've identified what unique skills and abilities you have that bring value to your employer, you just need to find ways to do more of that. You can try to focus on the things that create the most value for your existing company and try to negotiate a raise based on the increased value you're bringing to your company. Alternatively, you can find more customers that might value from your unique skill set. Your day job is your first customer, but there's no reason that you can't also provide that same value to another company on nights and weekends.

A Short Story...

I know one person that's a website developer that makes just as much money on nights and weekends doing side jobs as she does from her day job. She has simply taken the value she provides to the company she works for and applies it in other settings on nights and weekends. Since she's only getting paid for billable work on her side projects, she has to be much more efficient and can charge a higher hourly rate than what she makes at her day job. Where she might make $25-$30 an hour during the day, she can make $100.00 an hour or more at night for other companies that might only need to hire her on a very part-time basis. She didn't go out and try to learn an entirely new business, she just found ways to do more of what she's already doing.

How Can You Do More?

I understand that the advice above doesn't perfectly fit with every person in every situation. Some job situations, like being a med student or being in the military, don't lend themselves well to outside work. In this case, you either need to tough it out or find a way to forge your own path. Always keep looking for new opportunities to seize and keep asking yourself "How can I do more?"

26

A Networking Strategy That Works for Everyone (Even Introverts)

Every Wednesday morning, I spend an hour with 20-30 other entrepreneurs at event called 1 Million Cups at the Sioux Falls Design Center. I enjoy hearing speakers every week and pelting them with questions during the Q&A time. Before the event begins and after the event ends, there's typically 15 to 20 minutes of time to chat with other attendees. Honestly, that time is somewhat awkward for me.

As an introvert I'm generally not the type of person to walk up to someone (or even worse, a group of people) and start a conversation with them. I have never been good at walking into a social or networking event and working the room to find people to talk to. Although I'm not a natural social extrovert, I've developed a few networking strategies that work quite well (even for introverts like me).

One Year Ago

Toward the end of the last year, I realized that I was woefully unconnected to the community of entrepreneurs that exists in Sioux Falls and the greater I-29 corridor. I was losing out on a lot of valuable connections, potential business partnerships and investment opportunities as a result. I decided that 2014 was going to be the year that I would introduce myself to the entrepreneurial community in the region and beyond.

I didn't want to set a fuzzy and immeasurable goal of simply being better connected. So, I decided that my efforts would be focused in three areas:

1. **Having lunch and coffee with other entrepreneurs**

2. **Strategically attending and sponsoring local events**

3. **Producing content to establish myself as an authority in technology entrepreneurship.**

Strategic Dining

Like most introverts, I'm much better at having a one-on-one conversation than chatting in a large group. I figured that instead of chatting with a lot of people at once, I could simply have a lot of one-on-one conversations with other entrepreneurs. I decided that every Monday, I would ask three people if they wanted to have lunch or coffee "in the next week or two" (but mostly lunch, since I like to eat).

I started with people that were friends and acquaintances, then moved on to loose acquaintances and other people that I would meet at events. Since my book has come out, I've had an increasing number of people ask to buy me lunch, which has made the process even easier. Ten months into the process, I typically have three or four lunch dates each week with other entrepreneurs, ministry leaders and business leaders in the area.

I don't have any secret strategy to set up lunch and coffee meetings. I simply email or send a Facebook message to the person and tell them that I'm interested in hearing about what's going on in their life and business and ask if they are interested in going out to lunch. Prior to having lunch with people, I'll think about a few different things that I want to ask them about so there's plenty of potential conversation topics. After I have lunch with someone, I'll put a note in my calendar 2-3 months later to see if they want to grab lunch again in the near future. That's really all there is to it.

Content Creation

The people that are most interesting to talk to at networking and community events are those that have built successful businesses. People that "someday" or "might" want to build a business (commonly known as "wantrapreneurs"), just aren't all that interesting to talk to. I knew that if I was going to be able to network with successful entrepreneurs, I would have to establish myself as someone that has real business chops.

I decided to start writing about entrepreneurship and began writing one blog post every week. I also actively followed people on LinkedIn, Twitter and Facebook that I wanted to meet.

That way, when I ask someone if they want to grab lunch, I'm not seen as some stranger that probably wants to pitch them on some multi-level marketing scheme, but as the guy whose blog posts they've been reading for the last several weeks or months.

Attending Events

At the beginning of the year, I decided I was going to attend as many local business, leadership and entrepreneurship conferences as I could. I've attended a number of local conferences this year, but they haven't really been that great of networking opportunities. Since the focus at these events are primarily on the speakers, there's just not a ton of time to talk to people.

What has been very good for me, is the weekly and monthly meet-ups like Falls Foundry's 1 Million Cups and Think29's Entrepology. You tend to see a lot of the same people on a week-to-week and month-to-month basis. For weekly and monthly events, my only goal is to introduce myself to one person I don't know. I can usually even identify who I want to introduce myself to ahead of time by seeing who has RSVP'd to any given event on Facebook. If there's someone I don't get a chance to meet, there's always next time.

The Results

The connections I've made in the last year have generated tangible benefits for my business. Because I met Andy Traub at 1 Million Cups, I was able to write my first book, *40 Rules for Internet Business Success*. Because I was regularly producing content, Todd Kolb became aware of me which lead to a series of meetings that led me to acquiring an equity stake in USGolfTV. Most importantly, I've made several new friends and dozens of acquaintances as part of the process.

27

Why Your Personal Brand Shouldn't Be Your Business

There's an increasing number of people that have created profitable online businesses by building a personal brand. If you can become someone that people know, like and trust to talk about a particular subject, there's a ton of opportunity to create an income stream surrounding your personality and the content that you produce.

There are a lot of people that have done this very well in the last several years including Pat Flynn, Jaime Tardy and John Lee Dumas to name a few. They have blogs, podcasts and other content and make money by creating information products, by referring people to products and services to earn affiliate commissions and by receiving sponsorships for their websites and podcasts.

While I have the utmost respect for people that have built audiences around a compelling personal brand, that's not the type of business I would want to create. While I've built a huge audience (118,000 subscribers so far!) and a profitable company, you won't see my face or my name prominently featured on any of the businesses that I run. I could probably sell any of the four businesses that I have equity in tomorrow and very few of my customers would actually notice. I'm not trying to be anonymous with any of my businesses, but I think there are some compelling reasons to separate your personal brand from the brand of your business.

Here are a few reasons why my personal brand will never become my business:

1. **You get stuck on a hamster wheel of content creation.** When you build an Internet business based around your personal brand, your ability to generate income is tied directly to you producing content on an ongoing basis. If you stop creating new content (blogs, podcasts, etc.), people will stop coming. Your audience will expect you to continue to produce content at the same rate you have been. If you don't meet their expectations, they'll go somewhere else.

   That means you need to continue to produce content regardless of whether you're motivated to do so and regardless of whether or not you actually have something new or interesting to say.

2. **You can never sell your business.**
Whenever a radio host discontinues doing their show, the show is almost always scrapped entirely and replaced with a different program. Without the host, there is no show. The same is true for your personality-driven business.

The value of your business is the goodwill that you've built up with your audience throughout the years. If you're not there, that goodwill disappears. When your personal brand is the core of your business, it can't be transferred to anyone else without losing a significant share of your audience. This makes it almost impossible to sell your business in the event that you want to move on to your next product.

3. **It's very difficult to start doing something different.**
You and the personal brand that you create are inexorably linked. If you become known as the girl or guy that is the expert about earning airline miles and you make a great income doing that, you'll have a hard time transitioning if you ever want to do anything else. You might decide that you're sick of writing about airline loyalty programs every day, but your audience's attention is tied to you writing about miles and points. If you want to make something else your primary focus, you'll essentially have to start over with a new audience on a different topic.

4. **You can't systematize or delegate your business.**
In normal businesses, you can always bring on new team members or systems to improve how work gets

done. When your personal brand and your business's brand are closely linked, people will expect to be reading and listening to content directly produced by you. Your audience will want to read emails and tweets written by you, not your virtual assistant. You can certainly bring on team members to help, but you will never be able to build a team that fully takes over the day-to-day operations of your business.

What's the Alternative?

I run several different businesses, but my name isn't featured prominently on any of them. My name might be buried on the about page of some of my websites, but that's about it. Instead of making my personal brand the focus of my various businesses, I try to make the reader (or the customer) the focus. The writing style in my businesses will always focus on how the product/service/content impacts and benefits the end customer/reader. Instead of having a message of "Come, learn from me. I'm an expert!" the message is "Here's an incredibly helpful service or piece of content for you."

By separating my personal brand from my businesses, I know that I can always sell any of my business ventures if I ever want to. I'm not tied to producing content on a weekly basis if I don't want to and if there's something in my business that I hate doing, I can always find a way to delegate it to someone else, automate it, or simply stop doing it.

28

Beyond Revenue: What Matters Most in Your Business?

Many startups believe that fast growth and attracting investment (angel and V.C. money) are the two keys to their future success. They identify a high-risk, high-growth business idea, form a team and try to raise venture capital funds to build a product or service that addresses said need. They try to show growth as quickly as they can (often without regard to profitability) in order to attract continued investment. They hope to get traction and cash out by being acquired by a larger company or eventually having an IPO.

While focusing on growth and funding works out well for some entrepreneurs, it's not the best model for everyone. This model leaves little concern for the quality of life of the entrepreneur that founded the business. You're generally tied to the location of your investor and end up working in an office for 50-60 hours per week. You might eventually gain financial and time freedom after an exit years down the line, but that's the exception rather than the rule. If you're concerned about your quality of life while you're building your business, consider optimizing for other core values than fast growth and the likelihood of future investment.

Core-Value Currencies

"Fast Growth" and "Future Investment" are two examples of what I like to refer to as "Core-Value Currencies". For the purposes of this discussion, a currency is simply something that's measurable, finite and has value to you.

A core value is something that matters more to your business than anything else. Thus, a **core-value currency** is a specific metric that you optimize for and which shapes business decisions.

A common core-value currency that many lifestyle entrepreneurs focus on is time. They may only want to work 30 hours per week. This changes the fundamental question they ask themselves every morning from "How can I best grow my company?" to "How can I grow my company while only having to work 30 hours per week?"

Every future decision regarding your business will be made in light of the core-value currencies you select. You will make fundamentally different decisions about your business if you're optimizing for something else than merely top-line revenue. You'll be less likely to get distracted from your mission because you know what you're trying to accomplish and will have to say no to everything that doesn't optimize for one of your core-value currencies.

Examples of core-value currencies include the following:

- **Gross Revenue** — How much money can my company bring in (regardless of expenses)?

- **Size** — How big can my company get? How many customers and employees can it have?

- **Growth** — How quickly can I grow my company?

- **Profitability** — How can I make sure that I'm taking home the most money at the end of the day?

- **Efficiency** — How can I get the most amount of work done with the least amount of human capital?

- **Time and Flexibility** — Can I work on my own schedule without regards to anyone else's demands for my time?

- **Fame** — Do people know who I am, respect me and talk about me?

- **Location Independence** — Can I run my business from wherever I want, or am I tied down to a specific location?

- **Generosity** — Are we giving our customers the best possible value for what they're paying?

- **Resilience** — How long can my business run without me being directly involved?

American Consumer News, LLC's Core-Value Currencies

My company (American Consumer News, LLC) doesn't look or operate like most companies do. We've had a lot of success in the last couple of years (125,000 newsletter subscribers and counting), but we have no office, no regular working hours and a very lean staff (2 employees and 3 part-time contractors). We rely heavily on software systems, automation and outsourcing. My team members have the freedom to work where and when they want (as long as they get their work done). I'm not concerned about raising venture capital, how big my company appears to the rest of the world or how many times American Consumer News, LLC gets mentioned in business publications.

We also have a very simple business model. We create content and generate revenue from advertising and newsletter subscriptions—that's it. We're not constantly worried about creating new products, moving into new categories and businesses or latching on to the industry trend of the month. We're very focused on finding ways to do what we already do better through experimentation and split-testing. We're also constantly tweaking and improving our products and services to provide a better customer experience.

We're a weird company by any measure and I'm totally okay with that. Our core-value currencies are profitability, flexibility and operational efficiency. We're more focused on what we can take home at the end of the day (profitability) than what our top-line revenue number is. We believe that everyone involved in the company should have the freedom to work where and when works best for them. We also believe that anything that can reasonably be automated (or systematized) should be automated (or systematized) in order to gain maximum operational efficiency and a consistent experience for our customers.

What Are Your Core-Value Currencies?

No one can pick your company's core-value currencies for you. The core-value currencies you identify should align with your personality and your goals for your business. You should identify two or three measurable priorities as your business's core-value currencies and permanently seer them into your company's vision statement. Let your core-value currencies shape your priorities and use them as an evaluation tool for every decision made in your company.

Note: There's also a great episode of the TropicalMBA that discusses optimizing for core-value currencies.

29

How to Be a Lazy (But Incredibly Successful) Entrepreneur

Every Wednesday morning, I attend a local event called 1 Million Cups that showcases a local entrepreneur's business. I typically end up staying well after the event is over to chat with other entrepreneurs about their businesses. A few weeks back, someone I was chatting with made a comment along the lines of "Well, I won't keep you. You can't possibly have the time to stick around and chat given how busy you are."

Given the number of different things I'm involved with, it would be easy to think that I'm constantly working and have no free time, but that's simply not the case. My fundamental belief about productivity and work is that I should work as little as possible while still giving my business my best attention so that I'm free to work on the tasks only I can do and so that I have the freedom to enjoy the lifestyle my business has allowed me.

According to my RescueTime account, I spend no more than 45 hours working each week on the computer. I have ample time to play with my son, spend time with my wife, work out, read, relax, attend events and do other non-work-related things that I enjoy. I don't think that I'm a super-human productivity machine, but I do use my time very wisely so that I can focus on the tasks that matter most in my business and enjoy my life outside of work.

Here are some of the strategies that I use to run my four companies efficiently and effectively:

- **Work During Peak Productivity Times**
  We each have a daily measure of good brain energy to do complex mental tasks. For the first couple of hours each morning, I can tackle complex mental tasks reasonably well. After lunch, my productivity levels drop significantly, so I don't bother trying to work when I know I wouldn't get much done. I also know that I get a second wind around 8:00 PM, so I'll often work for an hour or two then. I also often work an hour or two on Saturdays and Sundays so that my good brain energy doesn't go to waste on those days.

- **Working on Your Business, Not in Your Business**
  Your role as the CEO of your company should be growing and improving your business, not running the day-to-day operations. If you're stuck in the weeds

of doing the work, you can't focus on building a bigger and better business. As soon as you possibly can, you should bring on team members (employees or contractors) to help with the day-to-day execution of your business so that you can focus on its growth. This point is emphasized in Michael Gerber's book, *E-Myth Revisited*.

- **Automate and Delegate**
  If there's an ongoing task that requires you to complete a specific set of instructions, you shouldn't be doing it. If something has to be done more than once each month, I'll create a standard operating procedure and have a team member take care of it. If it's a recurring task that involves data, I'll automate the task if at all possible. When you spend time working on recurring tasks that require little mental energy, you're not focusing on growing your business and getting more customers. This is probably the biggest key to the margin that I have in my life. I don't do recurring tasks and I automate or delegate just about anything that I possibly can.

- **Have a Simple Business Model**
  All of the businesses that I'm involved in have relatively simple business models. There are no physical products. There are relatively few products that customers can buy and there's typically only one sales funnel that involves getting people onto an email list, providing them value and selling them a product. By keeping your business simple, you can focus on improving the single path that enables someone to become a customer of your company without getting stressed out or distracted by side projects.

- **Cut-out Garbage Entertainment**
  The average American watches five hours of television each day. I watch about 90 minutes of television per day, typically during low productivity times (during the afternoon and late at night), as a way to unwind. When I do watch television, I don't watch commercials (if at all possible) and only watch shows that I specifically intend to watch (no channel surfing). I do however, read a lot of books and listen to many business podcasts.

- **Keep Email at Bay**
  Email is a monster that will destroy your productivity if you let it interrupt you throughout the day. I've turned off all email notifications on my phone and my laptop and check it as few as three or four times each day. The best way to work through email is in batches at set times each day (like before lunch, late in the afternoon and before bed).

- **Just Do the Work**
  I don't procrastinate on anything. If there's something that needs to get done, I'll add it to the bottom of my to-do list and typically knock it out within 48 hours. I don't use a lot of fancy productivity apps or "productivity hacks" to make myself more productive. I just put my head down and get to work on the task at hand.

30

Reduce Email Velocity to Make Inbox Zero Last All Day

A while back, I shared the strategies that I use to work through all of the email in my inbox and attain inbox zero (an empty email inbox). I use a lot of the same strategies that other people use to work through their email, such as checking email at scheduled times, turning off notifications, using Rapportive and combining my inboxes I usually do get to inbox zero every day, but it doesn't last very long because new emails keep coming in. Unfortunately, you can't stop new messages from coming in altogether… or can you?

I recently realized that I was sabotaging my efforts to get to inbox zero by responding to emails too quickly. It's very rare that an email requires an immediate reply within 10 or 15 minutes, yet I often feel obligated to respond to an email right away as if my inbox were an instant messaging service like Skype (or ICQ back in the day) because I'm naturally wired to get work off my plate quickly. In doing so, I'm encouraging the person I'm communicating with to send the next message in the email chain. Instead of getting 1 or 2 emails from a person in a conversation on any given day, I might be getting 3-5 messages because of my prompt responses.

If I want to get fewer emails from the people I communicate with in any given day, I need to delay my responses for several hours or as much as a full day. In other words, I need to reduce the velocity at which I send emails if I want to get fewer emails. One option would be to simply not reply to an email when I first see it, but that would require me to change my workflow. I'd have to remember to go back to it later and it would be cluttering up my inbox in the meanwhile.

Fortunately, there's a Gmail add-on that simply lets you delay the delivery of any message that you send. It's called Boomerang (if you haven't heard of it already). You can use Boomerang to schedule an email for delivery a few hours after you first write a message. You can also have an email sent the next morning or on Monday morning if it's a weekend. By using Boomerang to delay a message's delivery until the following morning, I (hopefully) won't receive yet-another-email in the chain until Boomerang delivers my message. This method also gives the other person, or simply the passage of time, a chance to work out the matter if possible.

Boomerang also has a couple of other interesting features. If there's an email that you receive on a weekend and don't want to deal with until Monday morning or afternoon, you can hide a message from your inbox and have it show up again during the workweek when you're ready to deal with it. You can also have a message automatically return to your inbox if the recipient doesn't reply after a set period of time (such as 3 days or a week).

I've been delaying the delivery of a good chunk of my messages for about a week now. I've found that it has reduced the amount of email in my inbox that requires a response considerably. This strategy won't stop new mail from showing up in your inbox, but it can significantly reduce the volume of follow-up mail that you need to reply to over time. The hardest part has been remembering to press the "Send Later" button that Boomerang provides.

31

Business Expenses: How My Company Maintains an 80% Profit Margin, Every Month

When I founded American Consumer News, LLC in 2006, I literally spent no money getting the business up and running. I didn't really have any money, so I started my online business using a free Blogger blog and zero-cost marketing techniques. After writing for several months on the personal finance blog I created, then called "Getting Green," I realized I would have to move to my own domain name and hosting account to take my business to the next level.

The cost was only $150 a year to get a domain name and hosting account with DreamHost, but that was a major expense for someone who was in college and still generally broke. I decided to make the purchase using my company's meager earnings and that was my first real business expense.

An Evolving View of Business Expenses

Having run a variety of businesses over the last decade, my view on business expenses has evolved. For the first several years, I was extremely reluctant to invest revenue back into my business. I figured that the job of my business was to make me money, so it wouldn't make sense to pay anyone to do things that I could do myself.

In 2007, which was my first full year of operation, I spent just $461.63 to run my business. This worked out well enough because I had plenty of free time to do all of the work my business required while I was in college, but it was a grind to do all of the work alone.

In 2008 and 2009, I began to realize that I could get more work done and free up my time by hiring out certain jobs. At the time, I was running a network of personal finance blogs that earned money from advertising. I got burned out after writing four articles each day for more than a year, so I hired a few relatively affordable writers to cover content production on my websites. This move freed up about two hours of real productive work time each day, which I used to explore new growth opportunities for my business. By focusing on the things that only I could do and having team members take care of most of the day-to-day operations of running my business, I was able to double my company's revenue in 2011 and again in 2012. That wouldn't have been possible if I wasn't willing to fork over some hard earned cash to contractors to help run my business.

While I've lightened up over what a business should spend money on over the years, I remain disciplined about how my company spends money. American Consumer News, LLC has been able to maintain an 80% profit margin for the last three years because I only spend money on things that either make my company more money or free up my time so that I can work on growing my business. It also helps that the marginal cost of the digital products and services my company offers is effectively zero and that I've identified some very effective free marketing channels.

Good Expenses

Whenever you spend money on something, it should make back at least twice what it costs you. For example, I can buy email sign-ups for my newsletter for $2.00-$3.00 each through co-registration advertising. I know that each email sign-up will be worth around $7.00 to me over the course of two years, so I'm willing to buy email sign-ups all day long because they're a great investment.

It's also generally a good idea to spend money on people and services that free up your time. As a business owner, your most important job is to continue growing your business (sales, marketing, improving processes, developing new products, etc.). Generally, you are the only person that can do that. If all of your time is getting eaten up by the day-to-day running of your business, you don't have time to work on growing your business. If you're able to hire someone to help lighten your workload and actually use that time for business development, you'll more than likely get a great return on your investment.

I have two customer service representatives on my team that handle 95% of requests that come in for any of my businesses. The work that they do easily frees up 3-4 hours per day that I would be otherwise working on the tasks that they do. They are a great investment for me, because that means I can start each day off fresh working on business development rather than starting off with 3 hours of customer service work to do.

Bad Expenses

If your company is paying for something that doesn't result in a positive ROI or doesn't free up your time, you should seriously question whether or not it's something you should keep paying for. A lot of businesses pay for things like office space, office equipment and supplies, furniture, yellow page ads and subscription services because they think that every other business does that so they probably should as well. Paying for things because your company has always paid for them or because you think that's just what businesses do is a recipe for low profit margins. Every expense should justify itself.

One thing that I've done to keep a lid on unnecessary expenses is to review everything that my company has spent money on during the previous month. I'll print out a list of expenses and cross out things that probably weren't necessary or a good idea in retrospect. I then give myself a score based on what percentage of last month's expenses I still feel good about. This exercise has helped me better recognize expenses that probably aren't necessary from the get go.

"Because I Can" Expenses

There are a handful of things that my company spends money on that do not make sense from a purely economic perspective. We sponsor entrepreneurship conferences and events, like StartUp Weekend, even though we don't get any sort of measurable return from them. My company gives out generous

Christmas bonuses and other miscellaneous perks to team members. I regularly buy lunch for new entrepreneurs and give them free advice. I buy better computer equipment than I actually need for myself and my team. While these things aren't necessary for the ongoing operations of my business, I feel good about doing these types of things because they benefit my team and the business community that I'm a part of. I have the luxury of doing these types of things because I've been disciplined about other expenses and pursuing growth opportunities.

Concluding Thoughts

You shouldn't be afraid of spending money on your business, but you shouldn't be reckless about what you spend money on either. Every dollar you spend on your business is a dollar that's taken out of your bottom line, so make sure that every dollar you spend will return at least two dollars down the line or otherwise free up your time so that you can focus on growing your business.

32

Why Some People Peak (And How to Not Top Out)

Why is it that some people peak and can't get past a certain level of success when others continue to grow and reach new highs? You might hit a certain level of income, build an audience of a certain size or attain a certain job title. When you try to move up to the next level, you feel like you've hit a ceiling and just can't get past your current level of success regardless of what you do or try. You might think you've attained the most success you're ever going to attain. You might think that you just aren't meant to reach the next level or think that you don't have what it takes to get to the next level.

Don't let this defeatist thinking hold you back. You don't have to peak at a certain level, but you do have to constantly change your strategies to grow beyond where you're at now.

You Have to Change to Grow

Let's imagine that you're totally out of shape and want to start running. You might follow a couch to 5K training plan and get good results if you actually follow the plan.

Now, let's imagine you want to take your running to the next level and run a half-marathon. You can't expect that the following the couch to 5K training will adequately train you to run a half-marathon (approximately 4 times the distance of a 5K). You have to run longer when you practice, do cross training, do strength training and take recovery days as appropriate.

In other words, you have to up your game. You can't do what you've always been doing and expect to reach a new level of success.

Do What Successful People Do

Between 2007 and 2010, I ran a network of personal finance blogs under the name American Consumer News. Regardless of how hard I worked and how many articles I wrote, I could never make more than $60,000 per year in that business. I tried to scale up the same strategies over and over again to grow, but nothing worked.

It wasn't until late 2010 when I started to look at what large successful financial publishers were doing to get good results and modeled their efforts. Based on my research of more successful competitors, I started focusing on investing content, building an email list and trying new traffic generation strategies. By changing strategies and modeling the efforts of successful entrepreneurs, I was able to more than double the income my business made from about $60,000 in 2009 to $139,000 in 2010.

Don't Get Complacent

After seeing huge revenue gains in 2010 and 2011, my company's growth stalled out in 2012 after a series of business setbacks. I had gotten complacent with the previous level of success my business had and stopped trying new marketing strategies and other growth techniques to keep my business growing. Remember that businesses very rarely stay at the same level of revenue, they're either growing or shrinking. If you're not actively working to grow your business, your business is probably shrinking. I received a wake-up call when my son Micah was born. I killed a bunch of side projects, doubled down on Analyst Ratings Network, tested a bunch of new monetization methods and new marketing channels. Not surprisingly, my business began growing again in late 2012 and in 2013.

Move Up The Value Chain

You only have a certain amount of time available to you in any given day. You do some things because you feel like you just have to do them, even though they don't contribute to your personal growth or the growth of your company/organization. These low-value activities, like mowing your lawn, cleaning your house, doing customer service work and doing administrative tasks take up a lot of time, but won't make you any more successful than you are now. In order to move up the success ladder, you need to outsource, delegate or automate these low-value activities so that you can focus on higher-value activities that will help you achieve your goals. If I want my business's revenue to double this year, I need to focus on sales, marketing, product development and conversion optimization. I can't get stuck in the weeds of day-to-day bookkeeping or doing customer service. I delegate those tasks so I can focus on the key growth activities which will take my business to the next level.

How to Up Your Game and Reach New Levels of Success

Remember that what you did to get to your current level of success isn't what's going to take you to your next level of success. You have to constantly change the strategies you're using to grow, model successful people, avoid complacency and move up the value chain with your time.

33

The Right Time to Quit Your Day Job

When I finally got around to quitting my day job two years ago, my business was already generating significantly more revenue than what I was making at my day job. Frankly, I waited too long to quit my day job. I recently had lunch with an entrepreneur that has an e-commerce business who is currently in a similar situation. His business generates slightly more revenue than he earns at his day job, but like me, he had a relatively cushy day job and the additional income was pretty nice. He is respected at his place of employment and doesn't hate the work that he's doing on a daily basis.

Like my former self, this friend is operating under the assumption that his total income will go down if he goes all-in on his e-commerce business. What I failed to realize (and what he now fails to realize), is that your day job will always take up your best energy and prevent you from working on new projects and ideas that will substantially increase your income. When you're working 40 hours per week for someone else, you probably just have enough time to conduct the day-to-day operations of your business. You don't have extra time to work on business development and growth projects that could be game changers for your business. When you quit your day job, you suddenly have 40 hours of additional time per week to work on blue sky projects that may not have an immediate short-term return on investment but could yield substantial results down the line.

I think this particular point is well demonstrated by the following graphic that shows my company's earnings and the income from my day job over time:

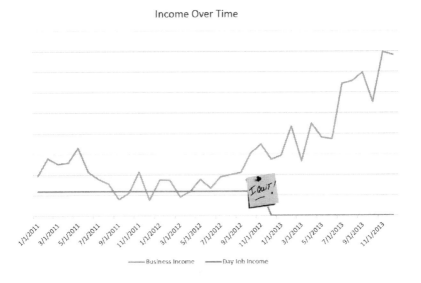

While there was a short-term drop in my income, I was making more than I was previously within six months of quitting my job. The numbers only got better from there.

What Happened When I Quit

After I put in my resignation with my former employer in November 2012, I suddenly had a lot more free time to work on growing my business. Instead of just keeping my head above water taking care of customer service and other operational tasks, I had a lot more free time to work on new projects.

I immediately began to pursue several new projects that have since taken off. I started working on my press release distribution business in December 2012. I revamped all of my opt-in mechanisms and display ads in early 2013. I started ramping up the volume of content my financial news business produces. In August 2013, I started GoGo Photo Contest with a couple of friends.

By putting a ton of work into a lot of new projects (many of which failed miserably and a few that were game changers), I was able to replace the income my day job had provided–and much more.

When to Quit and When Not to Quit

My baseline recommendation is that you should quit your day job when your business provides enough income to pay for your monthly living expenses. At that point, you won't have to worry about making bad deals or pursuing projects that you really don't want to just to make enough money to get by at the end of every month.

You have also proven that your business is economically viable and can create an income that sustains your lifestyle. When you make the leap, you'll have substantially more time to work on new projects and growing your business. Even if you think that you don't have a ton of different ideas to pursue once you make the leap, you'll have plenty of time to research and come up with things to try.

34

Sometimes You Have to Give Your Children Up for Adoption (In Business)

I used to believe that the best way to be an online entrepreneur was to have a portfolio of 5-7 different online businesses. Each business would be responsible for a portion of your income and there would be some level of protection if any one of those businesses took a nosedive. This is the model that I've followed until about 18 months ago.

I like the idea of diversification, so I've pursued a lot of crazy online business ideas in the last 10 years in order to create new income streams. Many of the ideas failed miserably, a handful of them had moderate success and Analyst Ratings Network skyrocketed.

The Danger of Side Projects

The wild success of Analyst Ratings Network left me with a conundrum. I could continue to start new projects in hopes of creating new income streams or I could double down on the one business that was growing by leaps and bounds.

For a while, I continued to create new businesses from scratch using the skills I had picked up from previous businesses. When Analyst Ratings Network was first taking off and hit five-figures in monthly revenue, I was contemplating starting a WordPress consulting business that might have made, at most, $2,000 per month. While I built out the WordPress business called WP Mechanic (which never really got above $1,000 per month in revenue), I was ignoring Analyst Ratings Network, my business's best growth opportunity. What kind of sense does that make?

Eventually, I got my head on straight and realized that all of the side projects I was working on (Matthew Paulson Consulting, Lightning Releases, WP Mechanic, Video County, etc.) were distractions that were preventing my company from growing. At one point, I had more than 60 different sites in my web-hosting account. It was hard to give up my side projects, because each and every one of them had been my baby at one point or another. I had big dreams for all of my side projects, but those dreams would never be realized under my ownership because of the limited time I had to work on them.

Complicating matters further, some of the business units I ran had active clients that would have been very disappointed if those businesses just went away.

Putting My Side-Businesses Up for Adoption

I decided that the best approach was to give away or sell my side projects. I effectively gave them up for adoption to other companies that could care for them and grow them in ways I didn't have time to do. The service businesses that clients relied on (WP Mechanic, Lightning Releases, Matthew Paulson Consulting) would continue on under new ownership to keep existing clients happy. Since these businesses are still operating, I have the privilege of watching them grow and flourish (but I don't have to worry about them anymore!).

The Adoption Process

I migrated my web consulting clients over to Media One, a local web agency that would serve them well. While some of my clients were sad to hear I wouldn't be working with them anymore, they were happy to know that they were being handed off to someone I recommend and endorse. I sold Lightning Releases to a couple of other entrepreneurs that can focus on and grow the business. Since my name isn't tightly associated with the brand of Lightning Releases, it was easy to migrate the business to their ownership with a minimal amount of pain. I sold the smallest of my service businesses, WP Mechanic, on Flippa. I also sold and gave away a handful of content sites I had built years ago to people that I met at Rhodium Weekend. There were only a couple of sites that didn't generate any money that I ended up shutting down. I'm down to about 15 websites in my hosting account now.

Continued Growth

I've sold or shut down four distinct business units that were part of American Consumer News, LLC in the last 12 months. Yet, American Consumer News, LLC's revenue continues to grow because I'm giving my full time and attention to my most successful business, Analyst Ratings Network. While it's only been a couple of months since I sold Lightning Releases, I've already replaced that income by moving ads around, improving my sales funnel, changing prices and making a few product improvements.

Optimize What's Working, Shutdown What's Not

If you have something that's working, focus on it and optimize it. Do whatever you can to improve your numbers on a regular basis through marketing initiatives and conversion optimization. The results will compound exponentially over time. If you make 5 improvements that improve your sales funnel by 20% each, it's not a 100% increase, it's actually a 250% increase (1.2^5).

If you run a business that makes $100,000 per month and a business that makes $10,000 per month, it only makes sense to put all of your focus into optimizing the larger business. You'd much rather see a 250% increase on $100,000 than you would $10,000. Arguably, keeping the $10,000 per month business is costing you money because it's preventing you from growing your larger business.

Focus on what's working, give up what's not working.

35

The Plagiarism Problem in Online Business

"What kind of products do you sell on Amazon?" asked one conference attendee to another at a lunch I attended while at Freedom Fastlane Live. Before the other attendee could answer, someone else chimed in and said, "You don't ask that question to another Amazon seller. Do your own market research." There's an unspoken rule that Amazon e-commerce entrepreneurs never tell anyone what products they sell due to the high-risk of someone finding their manufacturer through Alibaba, copying their product and undercutting them.

I've seen this situation replayed at conferences, on podcasts and in forums dozens of times over the last five years. Some entrepreneurs are deathly afraid of sharing any information about their online business because they fear someone will copy their business model and steal their market share.

The Rampant Problem of Plagiarism in Online Business

It's easy to see why anyone at an internet marketing or online business conference might want to keep their cards close to their vest. Any successful entrepreneur that talks openly about their business to the larger online business community will likely be the target of multiple copycats. Some would-be entrepreneurs believe they can't come up with an original idea of their own that would be successful, so they just copy someone else's business as best they can, hoping they can reach the same level of success as the person they're copying. Copying someone else's online business is rarely effective, because the copycat rarely has the skills to build and execute on the idea they are copying. Unfortunately, a high failure rate does not deter most copycats.

For example, my good friend Spencer Hawes openly built an Amazon affiliate site about survival knives to teach people how to build niche websites, only to be copied by several would-be competitors. After John Lee Dumas launched an extremely successful daily business interview podcast in 2012, dozens of other daily entrepreneurship podcasts launched soon after. I've personally had several people try to copy MarketBeat with varying levels of success, including one company that received venture capital funding. As best as I can tell, there are now 5-7 other websites that offer a daily email wrap-up of stockbrokers' research notes. Fortunately, most of the people that have copied my business really don't understand the financial news industry and haven't successfully marketed their products. There are a couple of competitors that have done reasonably well in their own right, but it's hard to say for certain whether they are taking a serious bite out of our business.

Is Secrecy a Competitive Advantage?

Secrecy can help relatively small online businesses avoid competition for a period of time. If you make less than $250,000 per year, you can generally fly under the radar and operate your business without getting noticed. After you grow past a certain size, you can't realistically stay hidden from would-be competitors. If you're one of the largest sellers of any item on Amazon, have the biggest AdSense account in your industry or are the largest affiliate for something like DirecTV, Proactive, or another popular affiliate program, you are simply too big to fly under the radar. Potential competitors will eventually take notice of what you're doing and begin to compete with you by replicating your business model. Success begets copycats.

While keeping your business model secret can prevent some competition early on, it's not something you should rely on as a competitive advantage over the long term. If the only reason that someone hasn't ripped off your business is because they don't know what your business is, you just don't have a very good business. You need to identify what competitive advantages your business has that will make it difficult for someone else to copy. If you have a unique supplier that no competitor can work with, you have a competitive advantage. If you have developed a marketing channel that would be very difficult for competitors to replicate, you have a competitive advantage. Try to build a business that has aspects that are very difficult to replicate in order to prevent copycats from ripping off your online business. Would-be competitors will still try to copy you, but they probably won't be successful.

MarketBeat has several advantages that our competitors cannot easily replicate. We have a better understanding of SEO in our niche than anyone else. We can produce content at scale. We have direct relationships with some of the best financial advertisers in the industry. We know email marketing better than anyone else and have a world-class software suite that runs our business. People have tried to copy parts of our business, but no one has been successful at copying our entire business because there are simply too many moving pieces for any one person to copy successfully.

How Copycats Can Help Grow Your Business

It was eighteen months into building MarketBeat (then Analyst Ratings Network) that someone tried to copy part of my business. I would expect my first copycat to be an internet marketer from an obscure corner of the globe with a lot of time on their hands, but it was actually a sizable financial publishing company that was our first copycat. We had been promoting some of their products as an affiliate through our daily newsletter. After receiving several sizable commission checks from them, they came out with their own daily ratings newsletter that looked suspiciously similar to MarketBeat Daily Ratings.

At first, I was upset that a partner had ripped off our newsletter. Then, I noticed they had made a couple of improvements over what I was doing, so I added those improvements to my newsletter. Whenever someone copies my business, I inevitably learn something and improve my business as a result. Any economist will tell you that competition is good for consumers, but I believe competition is also good for businesses themselves. I've learned about traffic strategies, data sources, ad-networks, opt-in tricks, and many other things from people that have tried to copy my business. I personally believe that my business makes much more money today than it would if I didn't have copycats and other competitors to learn from.

How to Build a Defensible Business

If your business is successful and is easy to replicate, a copycat will inevitably rip-off your business. You need to build a defensible business that cannot be replicated by a would-be competitor in order to survive and succeed over the long term. Avoid simple business models that don't take much work to replicate. Develop processes, systems, technology and relationships that competitors can't easily copy. Build a brand and acquire intellectual property such as trademarks and patents that your competitors can't use. Do these things well enough and you will effectively become immune to copycats. Even if others try to copy your business, you can view these attempts as a chance to innovate, always staying several steps ahead of others in your niche.

36

Why SEO and Google AdWords Aren't Right for Every Business

There is a computer repair business in the city of Sioux Falls called Craig Computer Service that is run by my good friend Craig Jurczewsky. I have been helping Craig with some of his marketing efforts off and on for the last six months. We worked on a wide variety of marketing strategies in order to attract new customers to his business. Social media marketing and advertising in the local paper worked quite well by making people aware of Craig's business.

We expected Google AdWords and SEO to also drive more customers to his business, but they didn't. It turns out that there just weren't enough people searching for keywords like "computer repair" and "virus removal" in the city of Sioux Falls to drive a meaningful number of customers to his business.

Not Every Marketing Channel is Going to Work for Every Business

For any given business, some marketing channels will work much better than others. At MarketBeat, we can profitably invest an unlimited amount of money at co-registration advertising and make a good return, but we have never been able to make Facebook or Twitter ads work.

An e-commerce clothing store might kill it with Pinterest ads or Google Product Ads, but probably won't be able to profitably run ads on LinkedIn or make a return on investment with a direct mail campaign. When developing a marketing campaign, identify the channels where your customers are most likely to be and focus on those.

Google AdWords, Yahoo Gemini, SEO and other strategies that place your website in search results are an effective strategies for businesses that people already know that they need.

If you're a plumber and rank first in Google for "Sioux Falls Plumber", you are going to get a meaningful amount of business because people use Google to search for a local plumber when they need one. The same would be true if you were a real-estate agent, a dentist, a heating and cooling repair service or an insurance agent.

If people already know that your category of business exists and that they need your service, they will search for you in Google and will find your business if you rank well.

If you offer a unique product or service, your potential customers probably aren't going to know about your category of business and will never know to search for you. For example, an acquaintance of mine, Nathan Rueckert, creates art using old baseballs. While he makes very cool artwork, very few people would think "Hmm. I'd like some art made out of old baseballs on my wall. I'll do a Google search to see if anyone does that." Another example would be my friend Laura Jenson that offers horse-guided professional learning sessions. It's an interesting idea, but no one will ever think to search for "professional development with horses."

How to Promote Your Niche Business

When you have a unique, innovative or otherwise "nichey" business model, you can't just put your business in the search results and hope that someone will find you. You have to identify who your potential customers are and go out and tell them about your business.

First, you have to get a good understanding of your potential customer's demographics and psychographics. What gender are they? How old are they? What are their interests? Are they married? Are they homeowners or renters? What websites, magazines and books do they read? Try to come up with a complete picture of who your typical customer might be. Create a fictional character (called an audience avatar) that epitomizes your typical customer. Give the avatar a name, draw a picture of them and write down every piece of information someone might want to know about them. Creating an avatar gives you a much better idea of who you're marketing to and how to reach them.

Once you have a good idea of who your customers will be, you need to go out, find them and let them know about your business. This might mean that you find a list of potential customers and reach out to them directly using direct mail, cold calling or email marketing. It might also mean that you find a website or magazine that matches your target demographic and advertises to their audience. You have to figure out what media (magazines, websites, TV shows) your potential customers are already consuming or what organizations, groups or communities they are participating in and then use those existing media channels and communities to get in front of them through advertising or community participation.

Promoting GoGo Photo Contest, The Quintessential Niche Business

GoGo Photo Contest is an extremely niche business that has a total of about 5,000 potential customers in the entire world. The business helps animal shelters raise money by giving them a platform to run online photo contest fundraisers. If you operate an animal welfare group, you probably would never think to Google something like "online photo contest fundraiser for animal shelters." Our customers would never find out about us if we relied on AdWords or SEO exclusively.

Since the concept is unique, we have to educate our potential customers and let them know our service is something that they need. We do this by acquiring email lists for animal welfare groups and pitching them on running a photo contest. Since it's not an organically-grown list, we just send one email per month to them to avoid being spammy or overly intrusive. We simply let them know about the features and benefits of running a GoGo Photo Contest. People come to our website and read our marketing content. If the service is right for them, they'll fill out a contact form. If it's not, they'll close the website, delete the email and go on with their day.

Marketing GoGo Photo Contest only works because we take the initiative to make our potential customers aware that our business exists and that it's something that they need. If you work in a commodity industry like web design, carpet cleaning or HVAC service, go ahead and do an AdWords campaign and try to rank highly in Google. If you operate a niche business, go out and find your customers and make them aware of your business.

37

Thought Leadership: How to Become Well-Known in Your Community through Content Creation

Three years ago, the name "Matthew Paulson" meant almost nothing to anyone in the Sioux Falls business community. I didn't go to any business networking events. I rarely made it a point to meet with other entrepreneurs and business owners. My name never made it into the Sioux Falls Business Journal or any other local media. Frankly, I was a nobody as far as the Sioux Falls area business community was concerned.

Granted, there wasn't any reason that anyone should have known who I was. I was a 27-year-old entrepreneur that just quit his day job as a web developer and built his business entirely online. This wasn't much of a problem as long as I only ever wanted to build online businesses that didn't require any human contact, but I knew that this wasn't the career path I wanted to head down forever. I knew then and still know now that MarketBeat probably isn't going to be the business that I retire with thirty years from now. If I wanted to have other business opportunities available to me, other business leaders in the Sioux Falls area were going to have to know who I am.

Fast Forward Three Years

In a period of about three years, I went from being a relatively unknown entity to a relatively well-known name in the community. I've been featured on a variety of local media outlets. I've been asked to speak at local events like Innovation Expo and 1 Million Cups. I've been asked to serve on boards for a variety of nonprofits and I get asked for coffee or lunch meetings at least 10 times per week. Falls Angel Fund, an angel investment group made up of 20 prominent business leaders in Sioux Falls, even asked if I would serve as the chair of the fund. I've had the opportunity to invest and partner in companies like GoGo Photo Contest, USGolfTV, Falls Angel Fund and Bird Dog Hospitality. I've made a lot of good friends, met a lot of great people and have made good money through all of the local connections I've made, but these opportunities only presented themselves because I am a relatively well-known and well-respected member of the Sioux Falls area business community.

Thought Leadership is Key

I didn't become a prominent member of the business community by accident. I did a lot of things to build my personal brand that you might expect, such as going to business networking and entrepreneurship events and meeting other business leaders for coffee and lunch. However, just about every well-networked business leader in the area does these things. The one thing that has really set apart the personal brand of "Matthew Paulson" more than anything else is that I've become a thought-leader of sorts on personal finance and entrepreneurship in my community. By offering my unique viewpoint on these topics through my blog and through my books and spreading them out far and wide, most of the people I meet for the first time in my community already know who I am.

Of course, this sounds easier than it actually is. In order to be a thought leader, you have to have some unique thoughts. You can't just regurgitate what Dave Ramsey has written and become a personal finance thought leader. You have to have your own unique ideas based on your experience. Much of what I write about comes from my personal experiences running the various businesses that I've launched over the last several years. I can also attribute a lot of my ideas to my life-long learning habit that consists of constantly reading nonfiction books and listening to podcasts. For example, it wasn't until I listened to an episode of Internet Business Mastery that I began to think of my email list as a core business asset. A lot of your unique ideas may not be original to you, but the way that you combine different concepts and communicate ideas will be your own unique creation. The key is to take what you've learned and present it in a unique and compelling way.

Spreading Your Message to the World

You might have the most unique and insightful message in the world, but that won't matter if no one hears your message or cares what you think.

First, you need to identify the types of people that you want to hear your message. Since I want to foster business relationships through my writing, the audience that I want to target is anyone that builds online businesses or anyone that's interested in entrepreneurship in my city. By identifying your potential audience, you'll have a better idea of who you should be creating content for and what kind of marketing channels you should use to spread your message.

You then have to figure out how you are going to reach your audience. You can't start writing on a personal blog and expect that people in your target audience are going to read it. You have to figure out the best marketing channels to reach your audience and use them to drive people to your content. For my audience of entrepreneurs, I've built a personal Facebook page to promote my writing. Whenever I publish new content, I put it on my Facebook page and use a boosted post to reach my followers and their friends. By spending a little bit of money, I can ensure that hundreds of people in my audience will read my posts. This is especially important locally. I can't count how many people I've met at local networking events that tell me they've read some of my content before they've met me.

I've also used a variety of other marketing strategies to spread my content far and wide. I've built up a Twitter following of about 5,000 followers. I automatically post my new content and content from thought leaders I follow to my Twitter account. I've built up a personal email list of about 5,000 people that automatically receive every new post that I publish to my blog. Finally, I publish ever new blog post I write on my Linke-dIn account to get additional distribution.

Developing Your Content Creation Plan

If you would like to use the content creation strategies that I've used to grow your own personal brand, follow these steps:

1. **Identify your content creation goals.**

   Why do I want to become a thought leader? What do I hope to achieve through my content creation strategy?

2. **Identify your unique message.**

   What do you have to say that's not being said? What's your personal manifesto? Why should people care what you have to say?

3. **Identify your audience.**

   Who are you communicating to? What kind of people do you want to be your followers? What kind of people do you want to influence?

4. **Develop your communication strategy.**

   How are you going to reach your audience? What marketing channels are you going to use to spread your message? What social networks do you plan on using? Do you plan on doing YouTube videos, pod-casts, blog posts or some other form of content?

5. **Create a content schedule.**

   How many blog posts am I going to publish each month? How often do I want to put out a new book? What is my publishing schedule going to look like? What time will I set aside to do the work?

Becoming a thought leader through content creation will take time, effort and consistency. While it's not the easiest way to become well-known in your community, creating and marketing unique content can be a fantastic way to set yourself apart from the crowd.

38

Let's Stop Playing "Fake It 'Til You Make It"

There's an old idea that if we pretend that we already are what we want to become, that our appearance of success will become a self-fulfilling prophecy. The thinking is that if we present ourselves as successful, then other people will also see us as successful and we'll have the confidence and the appearance necessary to actually become successful. Successful people want to do business with other successful people, so the assumption is that you need to appear to already be successful so that other successful people will want to do business with you. This is known as "fake it 'til you make it," but does it actually work?

How People Fake It

In the business world, someone who is faking it will convey an image of success that they have not yet achieved. They do this through their appearance (what they wear, what they drive, etc.) and how they speak about themselves. Entrepreneurs that are faking it will often convey that things are going great in their business and that they're generating a lot of revenue, when in reality they are struggling or have yet to get traction. Business owners might also present themselves as having more experience, expertise or notoriety than they actually have. Some faking it behavior, such as wearing a nice suit or acting confidently, is totally benign. However, faking it becomes dishonest and immoral when taken to an extreme.

Here are some extreme examples of people faking it that I have seen in my community:

- Telling people that they are making tens of thousands of dollars per month when they can't pay their own bills.
- Claiming to have a college degree that they don't actually have.
- Regularly dropping the names of extremely successful people to create the appearance that they have a close relationship with them when they don't.
- "Winning" an industry award that was purchased or otherwise made-up.
- Driving an extremely expensive car that they cannot afford.

Does Faking It Work?

People that are faking it in the business world want other people to like them, respect them and think that they're successful. Does this actually work? I don't think so. It's usually pretty easy to see right through exaggerated claims of greatness. In a world that's littered with Bernie Madoff's and Lance Armstrong's, people listen to claims of greatness and success with an increasingly skeptical ear. In addition, it's pretty easy to tell whether or not someone is being truthful about themselves with the sheer information available about people on the internet these days. For example, if someone claims that their business is upending an industry or changing the world, but there's no media coverage of that company anywhere, it doesn't take a genius to know that their claims of greatness are entirely imaginary.

If you are faking it, someone will eventually figure you out. Successful business people regularly talk to each other and word will get around that you're not being truthful in the claims that you make about yourself. When word does get around, you'll lose a lot of credibility within your business community. Others will listen to what you say with skepticism and will be much less likely to ever want to do business with you.

Even if you were to successfully get away with faking it, you would know in your heart that you are being disingenuous with people. You may begin to think that you don't actually have what it takes to be successful in your own right, which will sabotage any chance you have of actually being successful. Worse yet, you might actually begin to believe your own distortions of reality and begin to believe that you are already successful when you're not.

Let's Be Real

Let's start being genuine about who we actually are. People will like and respect you much more for being honest about where you're at in life and where you're going than pretending to be something you're not. If you're just getting started in an industry, that's entirely okay. Be honest about that. Others will love to see you learn, grow and advance in your industry and will celebrate your wins with you. In fact, there are many successful people that would love to mentor you if you're honest, willing to work hard and are full of enthusiasm. When you do actually become successful, others will celebrate your success because they have seen how hard you have worked and the progress that you have made.

When you do actually become successful, you should probably understate your success and achievement. Even if you are very successful, you shouldn't talk about your own greatness because nobody likes a bragger. If you truly are successful, your reputation will precede you and you won't have to tell anyone how successful you are. Other people will talk about how successful you are and that's much more valuable than anything that you might say about yourself.

CONCLUSION

Congratulations. You have completed your 38 day journey of reading through *Business Growth Day By Day*. You've learned about marketing, personal development, strategic planning, networking and many other business topics. I hope that you will be able to take some of the ideas and concepts outlined in this book and implement them in your life and your business.

If you would like to continue reading bite-sized business content on a daily basis, consider reading the 40 chapters in my first book, *40 Rules for Internet Business Success*, in the same manner that you read this book. You can get your digital copy of *40 Rules for Internet Business Success* at 40rulesbook.com.

If you would like keep up to date on my latest adventures and writing, visit my website at mattpaulson.com and sign up to receive email updates using the quick form in the right sidebar.

Other Books by Matthew Paulson

40 Rules for Internet Business Success:
Escape the 9 to 5, Do Work You Love
and Build a Profitable Online Business (2014)

Did you know that most "how to make money online" and "passive income" books are written by people that have never actually launched a real online business? Stop reading entrepreneurship books that were written by pretenders. Read *40 Rules for Internet Business Success* and you'll learn from a multi-millionaire entrepreneur that has created multiple six-figure and seven-figure online businesses from scratch.

Matthew Paulson, Founder of MarketBeat.com, has weathered the failures and triumphs of entrepreneurship for more than a decade. *40 Rules for Internet Business Success* is his collection of core principles and strategies he has used to identify new business ideas, launch new companies and grow his businesses.

By reading *40 Rules for Internet Business Success*, you will learn to:

- Throw away your business plan! Create a scalable business model that actually works.
- Identify a target market that is desperate for your company's products and services.
- Launch your first product or service faster by building a minimum viable business.
- Create a reliable and repeatable marketing strategy to keep new customers coming.
- Understand why most "passive income" business ideas are doomed to fail (and how to beat the odds.)
- Build systems that make your business run like a well-oiled machine.
- Maximize your company's earnings potential with the three keys of revenue growth.

Whether you want to learn how to make money online, create passive income streams or build a massive online business empire, *40 Rules for Internet Business Success* will help you turn your dream of starting a business into reality.

Get Your Copy of *40 Rules for Internet Business Success* Here:

http://amzn.to/28Ooy8T

Email Marketing Demystified:
Build a Massive Mailing List, Write Copy that Converts and Generate More Sales (2015)

While many have decried that email is dead, a handful of digital marketers have quietly been using little-known email marketing techniques to generate massive results.

In *Email Marketing Demystified*, digital marketing expert Matthew Paulson reveals the strategies and techniques that top email marketers are currently using to build large mailing lists, write compelling copy that converts and generate millions in revenue using their email lists.

Inside the book, you'll learn how to:

- Build a massive mailing list using 15 different proven list building techniques.

- Write compelling copy that engages your readers and drives them to take action.

- Optimize every step of your email marketing funnel to skyrocket your sales.

- Grow a highly-engaged and hungry fan-base that will devour your content.
- Create six new revenue streams for your business using email marketing.
- Keep your messages out of the spam folder by following our best practices.

Matthew Paulson has organically grown an email list of more than 400,000 investors and generates more than $2 million per year in revenue using the strategies outlined in *Email Marketing Demystified*. Regardless of what kind of business you are building, email marketing can serve as the rocket fuel that will skyrocket your business.

Get Your Copy of *Email Marketing Demystified* Here:

http://amzn.to/28XXqpJ

The Ten-Year Turnaround:
Transform Your Personal Finances and
Achieve Financial Freedom in The Next Ten Years (2016)

Do you want to achieve financial freedom, but have no idea how to get there? Do you feel like you just aren't making enough money? Are your personal finances a mess? Are you stuck in debt and wish you could get out? Do you feel like your current financial plan isn't working or isn't working well enough?

If you said yes to any of these questions, it's time for you to begin your Ten-Year Turnaround. *The Ten-Year Turnaround* is a life-changing financial plan that will enable you to turnaround your money problems and finally achieve financial freedom.

Here's what you'll learn:

- Grow your income by becoming an expert salary negotiator, starting your own business or doing a side-hustle on nights and weekends.

- Become an expert money manager and avoid the most common mistakes that prevent people from building wealth.

- Build a dead-simple investment portfolio that will provide a life-time stream of income.
- Learn proven wealth building techniques that allow anyone to grow their net worth, each and every month.
- Unlock the power of life-long learning and personal networking in your life so that career and business opportunities show-up at your door.
- Reduce your taxes, prevent lawsuits and eliminate financial risk from your life.
- Become a world-class philanthropist and learn how to effectively give money to charity.

In 2004, Matthew Paulson was a broke and in debt college student that earned $7.00 an hour working at McDonalds. By using the personal finance and wealth building strategies outlined in *The Ten-Year Turnaround*, Matthew was able to build a series of online businesses and amass a personal net worth of more than $10 million by the time he was thirty years old. Whether you're in debt or doing well, you can use the same personal finance strategies Matthew used to build wealth and achieve financial freedom faster than you ever thought possible.

Get Your Copy of *The Ten-Year Turnaround Here*:

http://amzn.to/28QNP4A

THANK YOU

Thank you for purchasing *Business Growth Day By Day* and taking the time to read it. Reading a nonfiction book can take quite a bit of time. Thank you for choosing to spend some of your valuable time digging through all the info I have to offer.

If you would like to share your thanks for this book, the best thing you can do is tell a friend about *Business Growth Day By Day* or buy them a copy.

You can also show your appreciation for this book by leaving a review where you bought it. To leave a review on Amazon, visit the product page at BusinessGrowthDayByDay.com.

Please be honest with your review and with how this book has or has not helped you on your journey to achieve your long-term financial goals. I want everyone to know if and/or how this book has changed your life in any significant way.

You can follow me online at my personal blog, MattPaulson. com. You can also follow me on Twitter (@MatthewDP).

You can also follow me on Facebook at facebook.com/ matthewpaulsonpage.

I am also on LinkedIn (linkedin.com/in/matthewpaulson) and AngelList (angel.co/matthewpaulson).

If you would like to hear me talk about various topics, feel free to check out the interviews I have done at mattpaulson.com/interviews.

Thank you and God Bless,

Matthew Paulson
August 1, 2016

ACKNOWLEDGMENTS

I would like to express my sincere gratitude to my many friends, family members, and business acquaintances that have encouraged me while I have pursued various entrepreneurial adventures over the last decade.

I would like to thank my wife, Karine, for being incredibly supportive, putting up with my unusual work schedule, and trusting me to provide for our family through my business.

I would like to thank my children, Micah and Adylin, for the many smiles they put on my face every day.

I would like to thank my business partners and team members, including David Anicetti, Donna Helling, Todd Kolb, Rebecca McKeever, Don Miller, Tyler Prins, Jason Shea, Stevie Shea and Toi Williams. Without them, my companies would not be where they are today.

I would like to thank James Woosley for creating the print and Kindle layout for this book, as well as producing the audiobook edition of this book.

Finally, I would like to express my sincere gratitude to Rebecca McKeever for compiling the chapters in this book, editing them for grammar and spelling and designing the cover of this book.

ABOUT THE AUTHOR

Matthew Paulson is a serial entrepreneur if there ever was one. His largest business, MarketBeat.com, publishes a financial newsletter to more than 400,000 investors on a daily basis. He is also a partner at GoGo Photo Contest, a company that helps animal welfare groups raise money through donate-to-vote photo contest fundraisers. Finally, he is a partner at US-GolfTV, a digital publishing company that produces regionally syndicated television shows and other content for the golf industry.

Matthew holds a B.S. in Computer Science and an M.S. in Information Systems from Dakota State University. He also holds an M.A. in Christian Leadership from Sioux Falls Seminary.

Matthew's first book, *40 Rules for Internet Business Success*, shared the principles and strategies that he's used to build a seven-figure internet business (and multiple six-figure businesses) from scratch. Matthew's second book, *Email Marketing Demystified*, provides a step-by-step guide for any entrepreneur to implement email marketing in their business. Matthew's third book, *The Ten-Year Turnaround*, teaches people to increase their income, build wealth and attain true financial freedom.

Matthew resides in Sioux Falls, South Dakota, where he lives with his wife, Karine, and his two children, Micah and Adylin.

Connect with Matthew at:

- Matthew's Personal Blog: mattpaulson.com
- AngelList: angel.co/matthewpaulson
- Facebook: facebook.com/matthewpaulsonpage
- LinkedIn: LinkedIn.com/in/matthewpaulson
- Twitter: twitter.com/matthewdp
- Email: matt@mattpaulson.com

Read Matthew's other books:

- *40 Rules for Internet Business Success*
  40rulesbook.com
- *Email Marketing Demystified*
  myemailmarketingbook.com
- *The Ten-Year Turnaround*
  tenyearturnaround.com

CPSIA information can be obtained
at www.ICGtesting.com
Printed in the USA
LVOW11s0513211216

518128LV00005BA/369/P